THE

NATIONAL

TEMPERANCE ORATOR.

A NEW AND CHOICE COLLECTION OF

Prose and Poetical Articles and Selections, for Public Readings, Addresses, and Recitations,

TOGETHER WITH

A SERIES OF DIALOGUES,

DESIGNED

For the Use of all Temperance Workers and Speakers, Divisions, Lodges, Juvenile Temperance Societies, Schools, etc., etc.

EDITED BY

MISS L. PENNEY.

NEW YORK:

The National Temperance Society and Publication House,

58 READE STREET.

1881.

J. ROSS & CO., PRINTERS AND STEREOTYPERS, 27 ROSE ST., N. Y

CONTENTS.

PROSE.

POETRY.

Contents.

DIALOGUES.

THE

NATIONAL TEMPERANCE ORATOR.

THE QUESTION OF THE HOUR.

How feel temperance men? How beat the temperance heart and pulse in reference to the emergencies of the hour? The day for declamation on this great question has gone by. We want facts; we want arguments; we want prayer to God; we want personal work; we want votes—all of them. If we get enough of all, we will have success; if we fail in any, we will fail in a vital particular. The great question of the hour is the question arising out of the decanter and the dram-shop. Some man says, "The question of the hour is the labor question." Quaint old Thomas Carlyle said: "The labor question as I see it is just this: that every man does as little as he can, and gets as much as he can for it." Friends, the true solution of all the labor difficulties to-day is not how many hours the working-man shall work, and on what precise conditions he shall work, but how he shall save his money from the insatiate gullet of the dram-shop when he has earned it. That is the most practical aspect of the labor question. Another man says: "The real question is political corruption—how to purify our politics." Purify our politics! Do you know that our politics have been rotted to the very core by the dram-shop? Bear in mind there will be no purification of American politics that ignores the bottle and the dram-shop. Another man says: "The question of the day is to reduce taxation." Who that is here does not long for the reduction of taxation? What is the cause of most of the taxation? The bottle and the dram-shop! Strike at these, and you have done more to reform political corruption, you have done more for the laboring classes, you have done more for their riddance from the burden of taxation, than by any and all other methods combined. And so I might start one question after another which men think to be the question of the day, and you will find this one underlying them all. I go further. I believe that the perpetuity and success of republican government in the United States of America depend more on overthrowing this master-peril and master-curse than any man of us, perhaps, can estimate or even conceive of. So let us as patriots, philanthropists, and lovers of our Lord and Master, that stand confronting this tremendous question, "How shall we deliver our whole society and the state from the curse of the decanter and the dram-shop?" look at it practically. The decanter is to be reached by personal persuasion, and by every man, woman, and child putting it away. The dram-shop is to be reached partially by that method, and partially by stringent legislation; for I hold it to be as fundamental as any principle of our Declaration of Independence that every community has a right to abate a public nuisance, and to express by its suffrage whether or not such a nuisance shall exist among them. REV. T. L. CUYLER, D.D.

IN THE CUP.

THERE is grief in the cup!
I saw a proud mother set wine on the board;
The eyes of her son sparkled bright as she poured
The ruddy stream into the glass in his hand.
The cup was of silver; the lady was grand
In her satins and laces; her proud heart was glad
In the love of her fair, noble son; but oh! sad,
Oh! *so* sad ere a year had passed by,
And the soft light had gone from her beautiful eye.
For the boy that she loved, with a love strong as death,
In the chill hours of morn, with a drunkard's foul breath,
And a drunkard's fierce oath, reeled and staggered his way
To his home, a dark blot on the face of the day.

There is shame in the cup!
The tempter said, "Drink!" and a fair maiden quaffed
Till her cheeks glowed the hue of the dangerous draught;
The voice of the tempter spoke low in her ear
Words that once would have started the quick, angry tear;
But wine blunts the conscience, and wine dulls the brain.
She listened and smiled, and he whispered again;
He lifted the goblet; "Once more," he said, "drink!"
And the soul of the maiden was lost in the brink.

There is death in the cup!
A man in God's image, strong, noble, and grand,
With talents that crowned him a prince of the land,
Sipped the ruddy red wine—sipped it lightly at first,
Until from its chains broke the demon of thirst;

And thirst became master, and man became slave,
And he ended his life in the drunkard's poor grave;
Wealth, fame, talents, beauty, and life swallowed up.
Grief, shame, death, destruction are *all* in the cup.

ELLA WHEELER.

RUM.

A SONG for the rights of man—
The day of his triumph has come,
And women and children have no rights
In this glorious age of rum.
Rum for the laborer's arm;
Rum for the scholar's head;
Rum for the man that lies in the street,
And the man that lies in the bed.
Drunk! drunk! drunk!
On Jefferson, Market, and Main;
Drunk! drunk! drunk!
Till the lamp-posts reel again!

The little girls have no bread;
The boys have no shoes to their feet;
The grate is as cold as the pavement-stones;
The father is drunk in the street.
Drunk! drunk! drunk!
There's whiskey at every door,
There's a palace for whiskey on every square,
But no shelter for the poor.
There is darkness in the halls;
The voice of joy is dumb;
And the graves, and the jails, and the lunatic cells
Are filled with the spoils of rum.

A boat has left our shores,
 To the Southern market bound;
But the pilot was drunk, and the boat sunk,
 And a hundred people were drowned
There was whiskey enough for all,
 But not a life-boat to save;
For the beauty of woman and the strength of man
 There was a watery grave.
  Drunk! drunk! drunk!
   Let the world do all it can;
  We will not barter our rights away—
   To drink is the right of man.

To the city fathers we call:
 If you have children and wives,
How can you turn your eyes away
 When we plead with you for our lives?
If you have hearts of flesh,
 Hear us, while we entreat
That you break the foul, deceitful snare
 Set for our naked feet.
  If you regard us not,
   And no compassion take,
  When the Lord demands your stewardship,
   What answer will you make?

Two Methods of Reform.

THE temperance reform, broad as it is, divides itself naturally into two branches; it is a reform of two methods. It is a reform, you know, in the first place, of the individual; it is a struggle against inward temptation; and then, as applied to society, it is a struggle against the outward incitement. So that, again, it divides itself into moral and legal suasion. We need moral suasion, of course, as the foundation of everything; we need correct public sentiment as the foundation of all correct action, and nobody can overvalue this. It is always to be present in our efforts, and nobody should think, if we make but little mention of it in our conventions, that we therefore ignore it. It is because we do not wish perpetually to go laying again the foundations. The foundations have been laid. We all believe in it; we all know it; we were all brought up to appreciate the value of it; and we do not wish to be repeatedly naming to wearisomeness the platitudes that have been repeated so often in regard to this cause. We know it all by heart; we value and cling to it, and we expect to as long as we are engaged in this temperance warfare. But out of this grows the necessity for legal suasion. I have a very short method with those who advocate moral suasion alone. I say, "Practise it upon yourself first. Persuade yourselves first to be total-abstinence men; for nine-tenths of the men who talk about this are not total-abstinence men themselves. Persuade yourselves, then try it upon your neighbor; then go hand-in-hand with those noble organizations that are lifting up the weak. Do the work of moral suasion; lift men up from the gutter; and then, depend upon it, there will be no man more earnest and pronounced than you in an effort to make the streets safe for the men whom you have rescued from the gutter." No man who has a Christian heart, who has wept and prayed over the victim of intemperance, and has succeeded in elevating him into the image of God, with a clean heart and a pure soul—no man trembles more than that man when he sends him forth to his daily work, to run the gauntlet of the legalized grog-shops that lie in his path; and no matter what that man's theory may have been when he started, he comes back from the work of benevolence indignant at the civilization that allows the weak to be tempted back to destruction again by this public incitement to vice and iniquity.

So that let every man follow moral suasion to the end, not with mouth and word only, but with the heart and hand, and I will risk his feeling upon this subject of legal suasion. HON. R. C. PITMAN.

ONE HUNDRED THOUSAND.

ONE hundred thousand men—
  Gay youth and silvered head—
On every hill, in every glen,
In palace, cot, and loathsome den,
  Each year, from rum, lie dead!
One hundred thousand sons of toil
Yearly find graves *in freedom's soil,*
  From rum, good friends, from rum!

On many a wooded plain
  Their glittering axes rung;
Homes for their loved ones dear to gain,
They tilled the soil, and plowed the main;
  They taught with pen and tongue.
Our brothers—living by our side—
They *tasted*—fell—and sadly died
  From rum, good friends, from rum!

Up many a fortress wall
  They charged, with boys in blue,
'Mid surging smoke and volleyed ball,
These they survived—only to fall
  From rum? Can it be true?
Once noble men—perchance our pride—
One hundred thousand MEN *have died,*
  This year, good friends, *from rum!*

One hundred thousand hearths
  Are rendered desolate.
And must it be forever thus?
Must children's children feel the curse?
  Friends, shall we vacillate?
Or shall our people now awake,
And with loud voice the nation shake,
  And cry, AWAY WITH RUM?

YE SONS OF OUR NATION.

YE sons of our nation,
Of every vocation,
Arm now for the battle
  Of freedom and right!
When true men are wanted,
No heart should be daunted;
For liberty's cause
  Let all freemen unite.

Speed on with ambition
True, sound prohibition,
And save sixty thousand
  From falling each year;
And all future ages,
In history's pages,
Shall tell the proud story
  To nations afar.

Shall earth's richest treasure
Yield to such sinful pleasure,
And golden grains wave
  Over valley and plain,

That malsters may gather,
To curse son and father,
That innocent joys
  Shall be theirs ne'er again?

Let malster and brewer,
And every wrong-doer,
Find callings consistent
  With God's holy plan,
And Satan's host tremble,
While true men assemble
To pass the good law
  That shall elevate man!

Then arm for the battle!
Let truth's cannon rattle;
And soon from his strongholds
  The tyrant shall flee;
And thousands now living,
In strains of thanksgiving
Shall swell the glad chorus,
  "Our country is free!"

Who is Safe?

It is indeed a terrible tyrant, the insatiate monster of intemperance. In the thousands of years that have elapsed since the sacred Word came from inspiration, every year has been realized the truthfulness of that series of striking and startling questions: "Who hath woe? Who hath sorrow? Who hath strife? Who hath babbling? Who hath wounds without cause? Who hath redness of eyes? They that tarry long at the wine, they that go to seek mixed wine." We speak of the horrors of war, and there are horrors in war. Carnage, and bloodshed, and mutilation, and empty sleeves, and broken frames, and widows' weeds, and children's woes, and enormous debt, and grinding taxation, all come from war, though even war may be a necessity to save a nation's life. But they fail in all their horrors compared with those that flow from intemperance. We shudder as we read of the ravages of the pestilence that walked abroad at noonday; but the pestilence, like war, kills only the body, and leaves the soul unharmed. But all sink into insignificance when compared with the sorrow, and anguish, and woe that follow in the train of this conqueror of fallen humanity.

My friends, from the most learned professions, from the bench and the bar, from even the sacred desk, this demon, like death, has seemed to love to choose a shining mark. Not the narrow soul and heart, not the one who clutches the pennies in his grasp, are the most in danger; but the genial, large-hearted men, who are not fortified as we are fortified by the determination not to yield to the first temptation. None of them are safe. From every profession he has drawn his victims. There is but one class whence he has never drawn any. The coronet on the brow of the noble of the earth, the grandest statesmanship, the highest culture, the most brilliant eloquence, have not saved men. There is but one class that has defied him, and will to the end. It is we who stand, God helping us, with our feet on the rock of safety, against which the waves of temptation may dash, but they shall dash in vain. I implore you to come and stand with us. I plead with you, for I believe that all mankind are my brethren. SCHUYLER COLFAX.

THE GOOD TIME COMING.

I KNOW when the good time coming,
  That seems so far away—
Such a distant, dim to-morrow—
  Shall be a glad to-day!
It will be when all the maidens
  Shall place beneath the ban
Of their indifferent scorning,
  Each tippling, drinking man.

When every girl and woman
  Who knows enough to think,
Shall tell her would-be lovers:
  "I wed no slave of drink.
No devotee of Bacchus
  Need bow before my shrine,
And offer a heart divided
  Between me and his wine."

If all the noble women
  Would tell their lovers this,
"The lips that touch the wine-cup
  Our own can never kiss,"
I'm sure 'twould answer better
  Toward helping on the cause,
And making men abstainers,
  Than half a dozen laws.

But if women will not do it,
  Why, then, we'll work away
With laws and books and lectures;
  But still I think and say,

If girls would go about it,
  Each, every one, and all,
They could sweep away the traffic,
  And crush old Alcohol.

Hurrah! for the valiant maidens,
  The maidens tried and true,
Who will not wed wine-bibbers!
  Are you among the few?
If so, then you are hasting
  The great good time to come;
If not, then you are helping
  That fiend and demon, Rum.

ELLA WHEELER.

I'LL TAKE WHAT FATHER TAKES.

'TWAS in the flow'ry month of June,
  The sun was in the west,
When a merry, blithesome company
  Met at a public feast.

Around the room rich banners spread,
  And garlands fresh and gay;
Friend greeted friend right joyously
  Upon that festal day.

The board was filled with choicest fare;
  The guests sat down to dine;
Some called for "bitter," some for "stout,"
  And some for rosy wine.

Among this joyful company,
  A modest youth appeared;
Scarce sixteen summers had he seen,
  No specious snare he feared.

An empty glass before the youth
  Soon drew the waiter near.
"What will you take, sir?" he enquired.
  "Stout, bitter, mild, or clear?

"We've rich supplies of foreign port,
  We've first-class wine and cakes."
The youth with guileless look replied,
  "I'll take what father takes."

Swift as an arrow went the words
  Into his father's ears,
And soon a conflict deep and strong
  Awoke terrific fears.

The father looked upon his son,
  Then gazed upon the wine;
O God! he thought, were he to taste,
  Who could the end divine?

Have I not seen the strongest fall,
  The fairest led astray?
And shall I on my only son
  Bestow a curse this day?

No; heaven forbid! "Here, waiter, bring
  Bright water for me.
My son will take what father takes:
  My drink shall water be."

W. Hoyle.

What will You Take?

How often this question is asked by men accustomed to the use of intoxicating drinks! Suppose we put the question in a more practical way? Will you take ten cents' worth of poison? Will you take a pain in the head? Will you take a rush of blood to the heart? Will you take a stab at the lungs? Will you take a blister on the mucous membrane? Will you take a nauseating sickness of the stomach? Will you take redness of eyes or black eyes? Will you take a tint of red for your nose? Will you take a rum-bud for your face? Will you take an offensive breath? Will you take a touch of *delirium tremens?* Suppose we change the question a little. Will you take something to drink when you are not dry? Will you take something to drink which will not quench thirst when you are dry? Will you take something to drink which will make you more thirsty than you were before you drank it? There would be some sense in asking a man out at the elbows to take a coat, or in asking a bareheaded man to take a hat, or in asking a shoeless man to take a pair of boots, or in asking a hungry man to take something to eat; but it is a piece of insane absurdity to ask a man to take something to drink—that which will not quench thirst. Why should he take something? Will it make him stronger, wiser, better? No; a thousand times no! It will make him weaker; it will make him idiotic and base. What does he take if he accepts the invitation? He takes "an enemy into his mouth which steals away his brains." He takes a poison into his stomach which disturbs digestion. Could he make a telescope of the glass which he puts to his mouth, and look into the future, what would he see? He would see in the distance, not far away, a man clothed in rags, and covered with the blotches of drunkenness. He would see a man deserted by his friends, and distrusted by all his kindred. He would see a wife with a sad face and a broken heart, and children growing up in ignorance and vice. He would see the poor-house, the penitentiary, the gallows, and the grave-yard within easy approach. Take the pledge, and keep it.

FOUND DEAD.

I AM weary, worn, and old,
  On the pavement hard and bare,
Shivering in the west wind cold,
  Night-frost silvering my hair.
    O rumseller! let me in.

Let me sit beside your fire,
  Give me just one sip of gin,
I will nothing more desire;
  See, my garments are so thin.
    O rumseller! let me in.

Once you used to open wide,
  With a welcoming hand, your door,
Greeting me with warmth and pride;
  For old times' sake, I implore,
    Good rumseller, let me in!

I had money once, and home,
  Wife, and pretty babies three;
They are gone; what has become
  Of them? I really cannot see.
    O rumseller! let me in.

Some say that I broke her heart
(Me? she was my joy of joys!),
That I did not do my part,
That the poor-house holds my boys.
O rumseller! let me in.

I have given you all my wealth,
Strength, character, all, all—
Wife, children, home, and health;
I am tottering—*I shall fall!*
O rumseller! let me in.

So the old man wailed and plead,
So he shivered in despair;
In the morn they found him dead
On the pavement cold and bare.
No rumseller took him in.

MRS. FRANCES D. GAGE.

INVENTORY OF A DRUNKARD.

A HUT of logs without a door,
Minus a roof, and ditto floor;
A clapboard cupboard without crocks,
Nine children without shoes or frocks;
A wife that has no bonnet
With ribbons and strands upon it,
Scolding and wishing to be dead,
Because she has not any bread.

A tea-kettle without a spout,
A meat-cask with the bottom out,
A "comfort" with the cotton gone,
And not a bed to put it on;

A handle without an axe,
A hatchel without wool or flax;
A pot-lid and a wagon-hub,
And two ears of a washing-tub.

Three broken plates of different kinds,
Some mackerel-tails and bacon-rinds;
A table without leaves or legs,
One chair and half a dozen pegs;
One oaken keg with hoops of brass,
One tumbler of dark-green glass;
A fiddle without any strings,
A gun-stock, and two turkey-wings.

O readers of this inventory!
Take warning by a graphic story;—
For little any man expects,
Who wears good shirts with buttons in 'em,
Ever to put on cotton checks,
And only have brass pins to pin 'em!
'Tis, remember, little stitches
Keep the rent from growing great;
When you can't tell beds from ditches,
Warning words will be too late.

ALICE CARY.

DOD'S SERMON ON MALT.

JOHN DOD, the author of this sermon, preached it under the following circumstances: Being on his way to London, he was met by some students of Oxford, who insisted on his preaching to them there, in an old hollow tree, from the word MALT. Having remonstrated awhile to no purpose, he entered the tree, and delivered the following discourse:

"Beloved, let me crave your attention; for I am a little man, come at a short warning, to preach a brief sermon, upon a small subject, to a thin congregation, in an unworthy pulpit. And now, my beloved, my text is MALT, which I cannot divide into sentences, for it has none; nor into words, for the whole matter is but a monosyllable. Therefore, I must of necessity divide it into letters, which I find in my text to be M A L T. M, my beloved, is Moral; A is Allegorical; L is Literal; and T is Theological. The Moral is set forth to teach you, drunkards, good manners; therefore, M, my Masters, A, All of you, L, Listen, T, to my Text. The Allegorical is when one thing is spoken and another thing is meant. Now, the thing spoken is MALT, but the thing meant is *Strong Beer*, wherein you drunkards make M, Meat, A, Apparel, L, Liberty, and T, Treason. The Literal is, according to the letters, M, Much, A, Ale, L, Little, T, Thrift—Much Ale, Little Thrift. The Theological is according to the effects it works, which I find in my text to be of two kinds: 1st, In this world; 2d, In the world to come. 1st, In this world, the effects are, in some, M, Murder; in others, A, Adultery; in some, L, Looseness of Life; and in others, T, Treason. 2d, In the world to come, in some, M, Misery; in others, A, Anguish; in some, L, Languishing; in others, T, Torment. Wherefore my use shall be exhortation: M, my Masters, A, All of you, L, Leave off, T, Tippling; or, 2d, by way of commutation, I say, M, my Masters, A, All of you, L, Look for, T, Torment. So much for the time and text. Only by way of caution take this: A drunkard is an annoyance of modesty, the trouble of civility, the spoil of wealth, the destruction of reason; the brewer's agent, the alewife's benefactor, the beggar's companion, the constable's trouble, his wife's woe, his children's horror, his neighbor's scoff, his own shame, a walking swill-tub, the picture of a beast and monster of a man!"

GIVE US GOOD LAWS.

WE pray for pure and simple laws,
  Tempered with equity and right;
Not statutes woven with the clause
  Which hides the honest fact from sight.
In every freeman's breast a spark
  Of patriot fire with truth ignites;
And traitors' hands upon the ark
  Are withered when the lightning smites.

For thirty silver pieces, told
  Into his hands, Judas of yore
Betrayed the Master; and he sold
  His own sweet peace for evermore.
Akin to him is he whose kiss
  Betrays constituents he scorns;
He crucifies with laws amiss,
  And crowns humanity with thorns!

When common law is common sense,
  In simple statutes plainly writ,
It is the sword and the defence
  Of all who wisely honor it.
The faithful legislator stands
  True as the magnet to the pole:
No bribe shall ever stain his hands,
  No perjury pollute his soul.

Now we, the sovereign people, plead
  For local prohibition laws;
Not dreary documents to read,
  Not essays on effect and cause,

Not points of order in debate,
  Not tactics of the partisan;
But just laws, for the small and great,
  To guarantee the rights of man:

Laws that will lock the public chest,
  And seal it with a magic seal;
Then, like the treasure in the breast
  Of honor, which no thief can steal,
Robbers will seek in vain to thrust
  Aside the bolt of destiny:
Their schemes will fail; for who will trust
  Them with the people's golden key?

"The good time coming" soon will come,
  When honest men with honest laws
Shall strike the bold rumseller dumb,
  And right, not might, shall win the cause.
Oh! then our land indeed shall be
  Foremost among the nations brave;
The asylum of the strong and free,
  Where stripes and stars in glory wave!

GEORGE W. BUNGAY.

THE TEMPERANCE MILLENNIUM.

THERE'S a shout along the temperance lines, there's victory in view,
There's a mighty army forming of the faithful ones and true;
They have joined the glorious host of Him that journeyed far and long
To receive his promised kingdom, and return with shout and song.

Through the long, long night of ages they have waited for the day
When the sun should rise in righteousness, and chase the gloom away;
Now, "Behold the Bridegroom cometh!" is the faithful watchman's cry,
And the glorious day is streaming all along the eastern sky.

For the crystal stream that gushes from beneath the throne of God,
Like an avalanche, shall lave the earth, shall wash it as a flood;
And the demon of destruction, and the poison of his cup,
In the grandeur of its flowing shall be lost and swallowed up.
Then the shout of white-robed millions shall re-echo far and near,
And the earth in royal plenitude proclaim the jubal year.
There's a shout along the temperance lines, there's victory in view,
There's a mighty army forming of the faithful ones and true!

GIRLS AND TOBACCO.

So you like the smell of a good cigar, do you? Well, I have heard young ladies say so before, but I always thought, if I was in their place, I would not tell of it. Whatever you may say, nobody will think you like the nasty, stinking thing for its own sake. Why, it almost strangles me. And after my papa has been smoking, I would almost rather he would not kiss me sometimes. I don't believe he would want to kiss me, if he should smell tobacco-smoke in my breath. I am sure he would not call me his rose-bud again very soon. I am very certain men don't like tobacco-breaths in other people. I wonder if that is the reason they don't kiss each other?

How do I know they don't like tobacco-smoke? Well, I can read some, and don't I see "No smoking" up around in ever so many places? And when I asked my papa what they did that for, he said because it was not nice to have tobacco-smoke from other people's mouths puffed into our faces. My papa said that himself. And then, on the ferry-boat, I see the men come flocking into the ladies' cabin, because their own is full of tobacco-smoke; but I don't see any ladies go into the men's cabin to get the smell of the smoke; and they don't scent their handkerchiefs with it, nor put it into bouquets. I should think, if they like it so well, they would have essence of smoke among their Cologne bottles.

Bah! nobody will make me believe that a clean, sweet young lady cares anything about the smell of a cigar, unless there is a man behind it. And the men don't believe it, either. They may not say so, but they keep a-thinking, and they think you say it to please them, the egotistical fellows! Perhaps afterwards they'll say, as my brother Bill said the next day after you professed to like his cigar-smoke—he said it made him think of the young lady that took a few whiffs now and then when she was lonely, because it made it smell as though there was a man around.

Little Ones Like Me.

When our fathers love the drink,
Madly drown the power to think,
Then they drive to ruin's brink
Little ones like me.

Wretched homes and meagre fare,
Filth, disease, and clothing bare,
Victims of these ills they are,
Little ones like me.

Warning by his course we'll take,
And the drunkard's cup forsake,
Lest his wretched fate o'ertake
Little ones like me.

Bands of Hope, like anchors firm,
Hold us in temptation's storm,
Bring to aid the world's reform
Little ones like me.

Like a fort when danger's nigh,
Like a rainbow in the sky,
Strength and hope these bands supply
Little ones like me.

Floats our banner in the air,
Its device, "Excelsior!"
Join our band, our triumph share,
Little ones like me.

Truth prevails, and right decrees
Conquest must and shall increase;
Bloodless are our victories!
Little ones like me.

Help! we cry, the foe is nigh!
Down with drink! Let tippling die!
Shout aloud the victory!
Little ones like me!

"Licensed to Sell."

YE who, regardless of your country's good,
Fill up your coffers with the price of blood,
Who pour out poison with a liberal hand,
And scatter crime and misery through the land,
Though now rejoicing in the midst of health,
In full possession of ill-gotten wealth,
Yet a few days at most the hour must come
When ye shall know the poison-seller's doom,
And shrink beneath it; for upon you all
Shall man's hot curse and Heaven's vengeance fall.
In vain ye strive, with hypocritic tongue,
To make mankind believe ye do no wrong.
Ye know the fruits of your unrighteous trade,
Ye see the awful havoc it has made;
Ye pour out, men, *Disease* and *Want* and *Woe*,
And then tell us ye wish it were not so;
But 'tis a truth, and that ye know full well,
That some *will drink* as long as ye *will sell.*
But here that old excuse yet meets us still,
"If I don't sell the poison, others will."
Then let them sell, and you'll be none the worse;
They'll have the profits, and they'll have the curse.
Bear this in mind—you have at your command
The power to bless or power to curse the land;
If ye will sell, intemperance still shall roll
Her waves of bitterness o'er many a soul:
Still shall the wife for her lost husband mourn,
And sigh for days that never will return;
Still that unwelcome sight our eyes shall greet,
Of beggared children strolling through the street,
And thousands, whom our labors cannot save,
Go trembling, reeling, tottering to the grave;

Still loitering round your shops the livelong day,
Will scores of idlers pass the hours away,
And e'en the peaceful night, for rest ordained,
Shall with their noisy revels be profaned;
The poisonous cup will pass, and mirth and glee
Gild o'er the surface of their misery:
Uproarious laughter fill each space between
Harsh oaths, ungodly songs, and jests obscene;
And there you'll stand, amid the drunken throng,
Laugh at the jest, and glory in the song.

Pour out your poison till some victim dies,
Then go and at his funeral wipe your eyes;
Join there the mourning throng with solemn face,
And help to bear him to his burial-place.
There stands the wife with weeping children round,
While their fast-falling tears bedew the ground;
From many an eye the gem of pity starts,
And many a sigh from sympathizing hearts
Comes laboring up, and almost chokes the breath,
While thus they gaze upon the work of death.
The task concludes—the relics of the dead
Are slowly settled to their damp, cold bed;
Come, now, draw near, my money-making friend;
You saw *the starting*—come and see *the end.*
Look now into that open grave and say,
Dost feel no sorrow, no remorse, to-day?
Does not your answering conscience loud declare
That your *cursed avarice* has laid him there?

Now, since the earth has closed o'er his remains,
Turn o'er your books, and count your honest gains.
How doth the account for his last week begin?
"September twenty-fourth, one quart of gin."
A like amount for each succeeding day
Tells on your book, but wears *his life* away.

Saturday's charge makes out the account complete:
"To cloth, five yards, to make a winding-sheet."
There! all stands fair, without mistake or flaw;
How *honest* trade will thrive upheld by law!

DR. CHARLES JEWETT.

TAKE HOLD.

A LARGE building had just been destroyed by fire. The workmen were soon busily engaged in rebuilding, and, as the heavy timbers were lifted to their places, you could hear the cry, "Take hold! take hold!" And the men did take hold with a will, and the building went up and up until it was finished.

Had these workmen stood idly by and paid no attention to the command, "Take hold!" the spot where the building now stands would have remained covered with charred logs, ashes, bricks and mortar, and everything would have been in confusion. But not so; they took their hands out of their pockets, and went to work with energy.

So, my boys, it must be with you. Do you wish to accomplish anything? Do you wish to rise to places of honor and respect in the world? Do you wish to be spoken of as one who has risen from the bottom round in the ladder of life to the topmost? Take hold. Yes, stop loafing and moping on the street-corners; take your hands out of your pockets, and take hold with a will, and soon, like the building I have just described, you will be going upward and onward, a beautiful structure—one that will command the respect and admiration of all men.

Do you wish to see the cause of temperance prosper, and the legions of darkness and despair driven from our earth? Take hold. Do you want to see the day soon come when whiskey will be drunk no more, when tobacco will no more pollute the mouths of your playmates, when the name of God will no more be taken in vain? Then stand not idly on the wayside waiting, losing time that is precious as rubies, but go to work; take hold, pledge against smoking, against chewing, against swearing. Will you do it? Will the young men of America take hold of the great reforms that are now agitating our country, and help push them onward to victory? God grant it!

THE WHISKEY RING.

"WE must have medicine," the landlord cries,
While whiskey-tears roll from his staring eyes.
"Without it, half our citizens will die.
All flesh is grass, and withers when 'tis dry."
It rains rum now, and yet there is a drouth
For ever in the drunkard's burning mouth.
Unparched by waters pattering on the roof,
Like oak-tanned hides, his lips arc water-proof.
His jaws extended break our laws, they say;
He keeps a rum-hole open night and day;
His open mouth, a most unsavory thing,
Reminds one of the New York Whiskey Ring.

SOBER REFLECTIONS.

IF I drink what is called moderately, I may be led, like many others, to drink to excess; but if I drink none at all, there cannot be the least possible danger.

If I take a little, others who follow my example, being weaker or not so careful as myself, may be led to drunkenness; but if I entirely abstain, I set an example which is safe for everybody to follow.

If I drink but a little, and keep a small stock for my friends in the way of hospitality, it will cost a considerable sum of money; but abstinence is a cheap system, and tends to promote economy among all over whom it may exercise any influence.

If I take my glass, I cannot reprove nor recommend my own example to the drunkard with effect; but if I am a total abstainer, I can do so with confidence and a hope of success.

Unjust Gains.

Prov. xxviii. 8.

"By unjust gain!" "By unjust gain!"
It was the rumseller's refrain
When called to leave his vast domain—
"*By unjust gain!*"

I felt no pity for the poor,
I drove them harshly from my door
While taking from their little store
My "unjust gain."

My goods an unseen Hand will deal
To him who for the weak can feel,
Nor from his pittance meanly steal
By "unjust gain!"

Now, as I go to meet the fate
Of those who hope to reach heaven's gate,
I'm haunted by the words—"Too late"
And "*Unjust gain!*"

Mrs. J. P. Ballard.

CHRISTIAN RESPONSIBILITY.

CHRISTIANS, patriots, men of humanity! will you not come along with us to their rescue—those who, misguided by the example and emboldened by the counsel of others, have ventured onward in a course which threatens to prove fatal alike to their health, their happiness, and their salvation?

Will you not, in place of casting additional impediments in the way of their return, contribute to remove those which already exist, and which, without such assistance, they will remain for ever alike unable to surmount or remove?

On your part, the sacrifice will be small; on theirs, the benefit conferred immense—a sacrifice not, indeed, without requital; for you shall share the joy of their rejoicing friends on earth and their rejoicing friends in heaven, who, when celebrating their return to God, shall say, "This, our son, our brother, our neighbor, was lost and is found; was dead and is alive again."

In view of the prevailing usages of the society in which you live, and the obvious inroads drunkenness is making on that society; in view of that frightful number of ministers at the altar, and advocates at the bar, whom drunkenness, robbing the church and the world of their services, has demented and dishonored; in view of those master-spirits in the field and the Senate Chamber, whom drunkenness has mastered; in view of those families made wretched, those youth corrupted, and those poor-houses, and prison-houses, and graveyards peopled—and peopled with beings made guilty and wretched by drunkenness—I put it to your conscience, Christians, whether, at such a time and under such circumstances, you would be at liberty, though supplied with wine made from the grapes of Eschol, to use it as a beverage?

In conclusion, I ask, Christians, whether you are not bound, by the very circumstances in which God has placed you, to refrain from the use of intoxicating liquors, of every name and nature, as a beverage, and whether you can, without sin, refuse to give your influence to the cause of total abstinence? DR. NOTT.

A MISSION.

SMALL as I am, I've a mission below—
A mission that widens, and grows as I grow.
'Tis to let alone cider, and brandy, and gin;
'Tis to keep well away from those potions of sin.

'Tis to make myself noble, and manly, and true;
'Tis to touch no tobacco, not smoke and not chew
That unhealthy weed that true women detest,
And all people know is a filthy old pest.

'Tis to say unto all, what I say unto you,
Let these things alone, if you would be true.
They are foes to all virtue, they lead down to shame—
Shun *drink* and *tobacco*, and keep your good name.

Cold water that comes from the well is my drink,
The healthiest, purest, and sweetest, I think.
It never makes drunkards, it never brings woe—
I'll praise it and drink it wherever I go.

ELLA WHEELER.

TEN REASONS

WHY CHILDREN AND YOUTH SHOULD SIGN THE PLEDGE.

1. IT will lead them to enquire what ardent spirit, wine, and beer drinking does.
2. It will lead them to resolve that theirs shall not be the drunkard's end.
3. It will teach them their moral and free agency, and that they are to be actors for themselves in future life.
4. It will cause them to feel, as they never have felt before, their own responsibility.
5. It will give them a new and permanent interest in the temperance cause.
6. It will preserve them most effectually from the enticements of the wine-cup.
7. It will prevent their being urged to drink by others.
8. It will make them good examples for others.
9. It will bring them out and embody them as a temperance army—a Band of Hope.
10. It will make them active and bold to gather in others and extend the cause.

THE TERRIBLE DRINK.

OH! the drink, the terrible drink,
Making each town and city a sink
Of misery, dire and fearful to tell
Of the numberless victims sent to hell.
Swearing,
Killing,
Crimes no lack.
The terrible drink makes night so black,

The curse of youth and decrepit age,
Adding to thirst instead of assuage;
Continual drink the drunkard's crave,
Till it drags him down to an early grave.

Oh! the drink, the horrible drink!
See the child from its father shrink
As he staggers home from the night's debauch,
Blindly,
Wildly,
Stumbling along,
Crazed with drink, intent on wrong;
And even the dogs, with a bark and a bound,
Growl at the man as he gropes around!
This is the picture, deny it who can,
Of the downward steps of fallen man.

Once he was free from the vice, but he fell—
Fell, like the angels, from heaven to hell—
Fell, to be mocked at, scoffed at, and beat,
Mingling with filth in the horrible street.
Pleading,
Cursing,
Dreading the worst,
Drinking still deeper, yet greater the thirst,
Till he sickens and falls, degraded and low.
Merciful God! in thy goodness save
Thine own image from a drunkard's grave.

King Alcohol.

The history of King Alcohol is a history of shame and corruption, of cruelty, crime, rage, and ruin.

He has taken the glory of health from the cheek, and placed there the reddish hue of the wine-cup.

He has taken the lustre from the eye, and made it dim and bloodshot.

He has taken beauty and comeliness from the face, and left it ill-shapen and bloated.

He has taken strength from the limbs, and made them weak and tottering.

He has taken firmness and elasticity from the steps, and made them faltering and treacherous.

He has taken vitality from the blood, and filled it with poison and seeds of disease and death.

He has taken the impress of manhood from off the face, and left the marks of sensuality and brutishness.

He has bribed the tongue to madness and cursing.

He has turned the hands from deeds of usefulness to become instruments of brutality and murder.

He has broken the ties of friendship, and planted seeds of enmity.

He has made a kind, indulgent father a brute, a tyrant, a murderer.

He has transformed the loving mother into a very fiend of brutish incarnation.

He has taken luxuries from off the table, and compelled men to cry on account of famine, and beg for bread.

He has stripped backs of the broadcloth and silk, and clothed them with rags.

He has taken away acres, and given not even a decent burial-place in death.

He has crowded our courts, and filled to overflowing our penitentiaries and houses of correction.

He has peopled our poor-houses, and straitened us for room in our insane asylums.

He has filled our world with tears and groans, with the poor and helpless, with wretchedness and want.

Smoking and Snuffing.

I'll never be a smoker, nor fill my nose with snuff;
Of practices so filthy I've seen and heard enough.
Snuff-taking it is foolish, and smoking, perhaps, is worse;
Some say the pipe's a blessing, but oft it proves a curse.
With vile tobacco odor the smoker taints his clothes,
And with a dirty powder snuff-takers spoil the nose.

These appetites degrading through life I will avoid,
And in examples brighter I'll try to find a guide;
No rational enjoyment in such habits can be found,
For the smoker is a nuisance to non-smoking friends around;
He wastes both health and money as puffing on he goes,
And the snuff-taker imposes a tax upon his nose.

Strong Drink.

The cruel wrongs "Strong Drink" hath wrought, the crime, disease, and woe,
The hearts and homes made desolate, what human mind can know?
Oh! count them by the drops of rain that from the heavens pour;
Or count them by each tiny grain of sand upon the shore.

Count them by the myriad leaves that wave 'twixt
earth and sky,
Including all the flowers that each summer bloom and
die;
Or by the feathered host that fills the earth with
songs of mirth;
Or count them by each blade of grass that beautifies
the earth.

Then take the ocean out in drops, and count each one
a tear,
Make every puff of wind that blows a human sigh
appear;
And then add up thy fearful list, nor look aghast, nor
shrink!
For it is but a shadow of the truth concerning drink.

Death and Drinking.

LIFE is God's gift. It is a great gift. We value it above all riches. In case of danger, all that a man hath will he give for his life. It is the period measured by Providence, during which all the pleasures and happiness of humanity are to be enjoyed, and all its duties to be performed. Oh! what folly to be constantly attacking, mutilating, and destroying that most precious of all jewels! Ninety-nine out of every hundred die sooner than they would by violating the laws of health and longevity, and a vast proportion do not live out half their days. Every unnatural stimulant helps to bring them nearer to the grave. Of all the other causes, the use of intoxicating liquor is the most powerful. Drinkers destroy the pleasures of life; nay, they cut off a great portion of it as effectually as if they laid their necks upon the block, and struck the fatal blow with their own hands. Nature truly bears up under a great deal of torture from strong drink; but at last it gives way, and often suddenly. Could we examine the progress of disease internally, we should be able to trace its insidious progress in every one who drinks strong drink even moderately. Indeed, an occasional bout of drunkenness does not harass the system near so much as the daily or frequent drinking of a few glasses in moderation.

Moderate drinkers, hear! The human slaughter produced by drinking is terrible. Are you not answerable for much of it? Do you not by your little drops praise the drink and favor the drinking system? And do you not, by this habit, obstruct the progress of the temperance reformation? For humanity's sake, do not murder yourselves by inches; and for God's sake, do not encourage others to do so by a bad example!

No Drunkards There.

THERE is a beautiful land, we are told,
With rivers of silver and streets of gold;
Bright are the beings whose shining feet
Wander along each quiet street;
Sweet is the music that fills the air—
No drunkards are there.

No garrets are there, where the weary wait,
Where the room is cold and the hours are late;
No pale-faced wife, with looks of fear,
Listens for steps she dreads to hear.
The hearts are free from pain and care—
No drink is sold there.

All the long day, in that beautiful land,
The clear waters ripple o'er beds of sand;
And down on the edge of the water's brink,
Those white-robed beings wander, nor shrink
Nor fear the power of the tempter's snare;
For no wine is there.

Father! look down from thy throne, I pray;
Hasten, oh! hasten the glorious day;
Help us to work as a temperance band
To drive the demon away from the land;
Teach us to say we will dry every tear
Which drink makes flow here.

TOBACCO.

THERE'S naught exceeds
The filth that from a chewer's mouth proceeds;
Two ounces chewed a day, 'tis said, produce
A full half-pint of vile tobacco-juice,
Which, if counted five-and-twenty years
(As from a calculation it appears),
With this foul stuff would near five hogsheads fill,
Besides old quids a larger parcel still.
Nor am I with this calculation done:
He in that time has chewed full half a ton—
A wagon-load of that which would of course
Sicken a dog or even kill a horse.
Could he foresee, but at a single view,
What he was in his life destined to chew,
And then the products of his work survey,
He would grow sick, and throw his quid away.
Or could the lass, ere she had pledged to be
His loving wife, her future prospects see;

Could she but see that through his mouth would
    pass,
In this short life, this dirty, loathsome mass,
Would she consent to take his hand for life,
And, wedded to his filth, become his wife?
And if she would, say, where's that pretty miss
That envies her the lip she has to kiss?

ONWARD.

ONWARD! onward! band victorious,
  Rear the temperance banner high;
Thus far hath your course been glorious,
  Now your day of triumph's nigh.
Vice and error flee before you
  As the darkness flies the sun;
Onward! victory hovers o'er you,
  Soon the battle will be won.

Lo, what multitudes despairing—
  Widows, orphans, heirs of woe!
And the slaves, their fetters wearing,
  Reeling madly to and fro.
Mercy, justice, both entreat you
  To destroy their bitter foe;
Christians, patriots, good men greet you,
  To the conflict bravely go.

To the vender and distiller
  Thunder truth with startling tone;
Swell the accents louder, shriller,
  Make the guilt enormous known.

Onward! onward! never falter,
  Cease not till the earth is free;
Swear, on temperance's holy altar,
  Death is yours or victory!

POWER OF ORGANIZATION.

THERE is always power enough to enforce a wise law, if it can but be organized and made available.

There must be organization for the enforcement of the law, with sufficient and salutary penalties. Good men must organize.

There are thousands of places in great cities where men drink frenzy by the half-pint, all of which depend for revenue upon the vice and misery they can create and the number of victims they can destroy. These shops must close, or misery and murder, debauchery and rags, filth and squalor, must haunt your streets at all hours and all seasons. They die fast, too, the devotees of the demijohn. Every year must yield a large crop of recruits, newly seduced from sobriety, or the venders' receipts will fail. They will take anybody's husband—yours, madam; anybody's son—yours, doting father; anybody's parent—yours, my dear boy. They will take them from you, hale, and fond, and true, and send them back to you bleared, and blasphemous, and beastly. They will blight five thousand new homes this year. Five thousand firesides will grow chill and cheerless, or there will be "hard times" among the death-dealers. And you must live, toil, eat, even sleep, under the shadow of a nameless fear. Your sons cannot walk the streets, or stroll in the parks, or visit the house of a friend, but you are haunted with thoughts that hold your eyes waking. Your daughters, if out of your sight, are on your heart like a brooding anxiety. You feel like men who know that a busy band of sappers and miners are laying casks of powder underneath their dwellings, and they know not the moment when their domestic heaven will be blown in fragments to the sky. It is worse than though cholera, and spotted fever, and black vomit, and the deadliest types of small-pox were to linger on every by-street and along your great avenues all the year round, pulsing in the poisoned air, climbing in at your windows, smiting the first-born in his pride and the babe in the cradle, keeping the sick-lamp for ever burning like a pale star in every habitation.

Oh! are we to live on in this mortal peril? Are we always to stand in dread of a great calamity? Are we so enslaved, so torpid, so timorous? Who will make common cause against the most insidious and malignant foe to our peace and our liberties? Come as with one impulse, fair women and brave men, all who dare to be right and true. Duty and danger, love and law, patriotism and philanthropy, call us. Let us support sentiment and advice with the emphasis of a faultless example.

REV. M. C. BRIGGS.

THE LITTLE SHOES.

SOME months ago—I need not mention where—
There was a meeting in a temperance hall,
And many a working-man assembled there;
Among them sat a man, well dressed and tall,
Who listened anxiously to every word,
Until one near spoke to him thus:
"Come, William Turner, I have never heard
How that you changed so much; so tell to us
Why you gave up the public-house? Ah! few,
I'm sure, can tell so strange a tale as you."

Up rose William at the summons,
  Glanced confusedly round the hall,
Cried, with voice of deep emotion,
  "The little shoes—they did it all!

"One night, on the verge of ruin,
  As I hurried from the tap,
I beheld the landlord's baby
  Sitting in its mother's lap.

"'Look, dear father,' said the mother
  Holding forth the little feet;
'Look, we've got new shoes for darling!
  Don't you think them nice and neat?'

"Ye may judge the thing is simple,
  Disbelieve me if you choose;
But, my friends, no fist e'er struck me
  Such a blow as those small shoes.

"And they forced my brain to reason:
  'What right,' said I, standing there,
'Have I to clothe another's children,
  And to let my own go bare?

"It was in the depth of winter,
  Bitter was the night, and wild;
And outside the flaring gin-shop
  Stood my starving wife and child.

"Out I went, and clutched my baby,
  Saw its feet so cold and blue;
Fathers! if the small shoes smote me,
  What did those poor bare feet do?

"Quick I thrust them in my bosom;
  Oh! they were so icy chill!
And their coldness, like a dagger,
  Pierced me—I can feel it still.

"Of money I had but a trifle,
  Just enough to serve my stead;
It bought shoes for little baby
  And a single loaf of bread.

"That loaf served us all the Sunday,
  And I went to work next day.
Since that time I've been teetotal—
  That is all I've got to say."

Anti-Catawba.

REPLY TO LONGFELLOW'S "CATAWBA WINE."

Poet Longfellow sings, in his lyric for kings,
  The praise of Catawba wine;
Catawba, he thinks, is the nectar of drinks,
  An elixir—semi-divine.

Did it ne'er strike the poet—if not, he should know it—
  Though bards are not always deep thinkers,
That wine, as the first step, is often the worst step
  That's taken by alcohol drinkers.

No song will I sing you, no wreath will I bring you,
  Ensanguined with blood of the vine;
The ruby-red bowl, death to body and soul,
  Shall be eulogy, never, of mine!

For many a mother, wife, sister, and brother,
The past and the present reviewing,
Can trace to red wine, that fell spirit malign,
That led to a loved one's undoing.

Then sing no more verses whose sweet sound rehearses
The praise of Catawba wine;
Sing of beauty and flowers, and rosy-wreathed bowers,
But not of the juice of the vine!

Sing the praises of water—earth's diamond-eyed daughter,
The belle of the elements too—
Of moss-covered fountains, of forest-clad mountains,
Of faith, hope, and charity too!

Sing the death-wail of battle, whilst war's dying rattle
Sinks deep to the doom that it merits;
And peace, all victorious, rises sun-like and glorious,
To reign o'er the land she inherits!

Great bard of our nation! men yield thee oblation,
Fame's laurels thy temples entwine;
Add still to thy glory, live ever in story,
But not in thy song to the vine!

JOSEPH MERREFIELD.

AGITATE; OR, THE TWO MASTERS.

AGITATION is the only lever of this century; it is the great engineer of the time. It is the grand dynamic force by which the whole people are to be lifted up to a higher and a nobler level—the level of honorable self-respect, the result of self-control. The people are always right in the long run. You may deceive them for a time; their own appetites and their own passions may lead them astray for a while; but the moment you set the American people thinking, you set them in that straight and narrow path which leads to the Zion that lies before. Now, we have had two masters in our country, and they have ruled us for a long while with an iron hand. We have been terribly afraid of their grim visages. The one is dead and buried. He was dethroned some years ago. He was dethroned when Lee gave the handle of his sword to General Grant. You could hear the clank of his chain all over the South; it was the slavery of the body, as well as that of the mind and soul. The din of its harsh music reached our ears, and for many, many years we agitated and agitated, setting this audience to thinking now, and to-morrow that audience; some of our apostles being sealed and ordained to their work by the ministries of Croton, brickbats, and rotten eggs; but at last the mine was fired, at last the explosion came, at last a million of freemen in the North took it into their own hands, and, dressing into line, walked from the Ohio to the Gulf, and left behind them only freemen wherever they trod! The chains dropped; and now the country has forgotten the clank of the chain, and it remembers only that it has inscribed upon the folds of its flag the better, nobler, and grander word—LIBERTY! But there is another master remaining. It was a double throne that ruled us; it was a double tyranny to which we bowed. One tyrant has descended, his throne is levelled with the earth; but the other sits there. The other frowns from his lordly palace; the other utters from his iron, sarcastic lips those words which were uttered by one of your public officials a few months since, "What are you going to do about it?" We answered that question months ago. We propose to answer the next question in the course of a few months. The tyrant who now sits enthroned shall follow in the wake of the tyrants who have been dethroned. Ours is a work the result of which is a "God bless you!" heaped upon some prayerful apostle; the "God bless you!" coming from widows hearts, coming from orphans' lips, coming from men who are redeemed from drunkenness and lifted up to the higher level of their noblest manhood! Now, what we are trying to do is simply to match the devil; we are trying to work in the line of God's eternal providence; we are trying to work in the divine line of the teaching of the Sermon on the Mount; we are trying to teach the world that

"A man's a man for a' that;"

that it is not poverty which disgraces a man, that it is not always wealth which honors a man, that there is a nobility on the earth, and there is a nobility in the midst of our republic. He is noble who controls himself; he is noble who holds himself well in hand, and, like a blood horse, is doing his utmost and saving his strength going along the high-road to win the race at last. That is the object which we have in view, and the only one; and every man who signs the pledge and keeps it cheats the devil, while the angels praise God and say, "Our brother was lost, and is found; our brother was dead, but now he is alive again." REV. GEO. H. HEPWORTH.

WORK AND PRAY.

THERE'S a feeling stronger growing;
Push away!
There's a stream of reason flowing;
Work and pray;
There's a spirit having birth,
Robed in truth and moral worth,
That shall purify the earth
In the future day.

Aid the movement, every preacher;
Push away!
Aid it, every Sunday teacher;
Work and pray;
Aid it, hosts of Christian men,
Pulpit, platform, press, and pen,
Eden's flowers shall bloom again
In the future day.

Aid it, every wisdom-seeker;
Push away!
Strong drink's power is growing weaker;
Work and pray;
Work! the happy era nears
That shall stay its groans and fears;
There will be no drink-caused tears
In the future day.

Help! they are your erring neighbors
Led astray.
Heaven is smiling on your labors;
Work and pray;
Help the paradise to make,
Help! for human life's at stake,
Help! oh! help for mercy's sake
On the happier day.

Wine is a Mocker.

THERE is a mocker, aged and diseased,
Yet with him still are all the nations pleased;
He hath a charm for sickness and for health,
For heat or cold, for poverty or wealth.
When grandeur asks him in her stately rooms,
A foreign name and title he assumes;

When plebeians call their common friend to see
His plain appellative begins with B (beer);
And yet, despite his *price*, or *age*, or *name*,
The spirit that inspires him is the same.
Accursed spirit! that throughout all time
Hath been the friend of every flagrant crime,
Is there a villain who would dare proceed
Without its aid to do some fearful deed?
Is there recorded one more shameful blot
Of deepest dye, and this foul fiend was not?
Hark! there ascends a sad, despairing cry
From those who have been duped and slain thereby
"*Look not upon it!*" Inspiration writes:
"At last the adder stings, the serpent bites."
"*Wine is a mocker!*" If that still be true,
Its modern substitutes are mockers too.

A Moderate Drinker's Soliloquy.

I own I am shocked at the traffic in drink;
Of all our sad sights, 'tis the saddest, I think,
To see men besotted, betrayed, and degraded,
Their happiness blighted, their reason invaded.

I wish it were altered, but *I* can't begin;
For how can I give up my brandy and gin?
Especially brandy, so useful, you see—
What! give up our spirits, and only drink tea?

Besides, if I do, the neighbors will say,
"He's turned a teetotaler; we'd best stop away."
They'll laugh at my scruples, and call me a flat;
And I can bear *anything* rather than that.

If Brown, Jones, and Robinson all would agree
To give up the drink, 'twould be easy for me;
But whilst they keep mixing and taking a drop,
I don't see why *I* should be called on to stop.

It is true that Brown's nose is exceedingly red,
But he says that the drink never gets to his head;
And that's very likely, for I should suppose
It can't reach his brain if it stops at his nose.

And Jones has been having a touch of the gout,
And finds it an effort to hobble about;
It's strange if the mixture that reddens Brown's nose
Should also be found to affect Jones's toes.

And Robinson lately has had an affection
That's given his features a golden complexion;
And the doctor declares he's had brandy enough,
And prescribes for his case "Aqua Pura, Quant. Suff."

If the evils of drinking alike can be seen
In the face, in the feet, in the liver and spleen,
Spite of B., J. and R. an abstainer I'll be,
And no one shall ever learn drinking from me.

R. Hooper.

The Rottenness of Moderation.

Now, there are some who cannot drink moderately; therefore, moderation is not a safe example for all. Then you will draw the line somewhere? Yes, those who cannot drink moderately must give it up. Then we say to you who can drink moderately, will you give it up to help them? That is the point. It is hard for some young men to give it up, and bear the sneers, and shrugs, and laughter. One said to me, "I would rather stand up and run the risk of a rifle-bullet at a hundred paces than stand the jeers of my comrades in the barrack-room." There is many a man in this room who would not dare to kneel down beside his bed and do as his mother taught him when a boy, if half a dozen jeering, ungodly, witty companions were present. Why? He is afraid of them! Afraid of what? Afraid of the laughter! How is it? A young man goes into society; he feels he is drinking too much; he feels he is one of those who can't stand it; he feels that its influence on the brain is fascinating, and he gets bewildered by it. In the morning, when, perhaps, he kneels and asks God's blessing on him for the day, he says, "I will be careful; I will be careful." Why not give it up altogether, sir? There is the pinch. He goes into society. Perhaps some young men meet together. "Well, Charley, how d'ye do?" "I'm pretty well." "Will you have a glass of wine? Here are five or six of us taking a glass; won't you join us?" He wants it. The appetite is forming. He would like it. He knows its exhilarations, but he says, "No, I thank you; I will not take it." "Not take it? What is the matter with you? Are you ill?" "Oh! no, I am not ill." "Come and take a glass with us." He wants it. 'No, no, thank you, the fact is, I've—" They all have their glasses in their hands, and he is sensitive. He shrinks from anything like ridicule. "No," he says, "I have decided that I won't drink any more." "What! you have been and joined the teetotalers? Well, upon my word! Are you—are you—are you a teetotaler?" Now, sir, you said teetotalers are cowards. It requires more moral courage than some of you have got to stand up with half a dozen drinking young men, and say, "I am a teetotaler." Let him say it, and what then? He will hear the laugh, "Ah! ah! ah! Well, really, we shall have you with a medal and a blue ribbon by-and-by! Have you joined the Band of Hope? Oh! ah! yes; go along with you! Well, it is a very good thing for a man if he cannot govern himself. It is the best thing a man can do if he is weak-minded. If I were a weak-minded man, and could not govern myself, I would be a teetotaler; but you and I, Jim, and Dick, and Tom, can take care of ourselves; there is a poor fellow that cannot." Do you suppose he will stand that? I don't expect to make all teetotalers that hear me now; but if I can say one word to induce you to keep back the sneer when you see a man adopt a safe principle for his own sake, I shall be thankful. If I cannot make you teetotalers, if I can induce you to lay your hand on the shoulder of the next young man that in company refuses to drink wine, and to say, "That is right, my man; it is a safe principle!" then it will be worth all the effort; for young men are kept out of the movement more by the fear of ridicule than even by their love of drink up to a certain point.

JOHN B. GOUGH.

WIDE AWAKE.

THERE'S a labor to be wrought,
  There's a race that we must run,
There's a battle to be fought,
  And a victory to be won
For a cheated nation's sake!
  Ho! ye people, plundered all
  By the slaves of alcohol,
Rouse, the demon's arm to break;
Wide awake, boys! wide awake!

In the councils of the great,
  In the hovels of the low,
In the very halls of state,
  Sits the desolating foe;

Only human life can slake
  His infernal thirst for blood;
  Up, ye virtuous brotherhood,
Smite him till his vassals quake;
Wide awake, boys! wide awake!

See him, in the holy place,
  Lurking in the blessed wine;
Glancing through the bridal lace,
  How his deadly eyeballs shine!
Coiling like a venomed snake
  In the parlor's social ring,
  Strength and beauty feel his sting.
Hurl him to his burning lake!
Wide awake, boys! wide awake!

Where the dens of haggard crime
  Draw the wretch to deeper shame,
Loathsome in his evil slime,
  Blacker vices than we name
Of the demon's cup partake;
  All his garnered fruits are there,
  Bathing in the poisoned air.
Through his fen quick clearance make;
Wide awake, boys! wide awake!

GEO. S. BURLEIGH.

THE CRY OF THE EARTH.

"O GOD!" sighs the grain, as it goldens the hills,
  And waves, like the sea, in the meadows below,
"Oh! why should I poison the stream in the stills?
  Or change the pure water to currents of woe?"

"Why," murmurs the corn on the slopes of the plains,
"Should my sweetness and strength be perverted to crime?
My health-giving juices be tortured to pains?
My nurture be tainted with fetor and slime?"

"Ah!" moan the rich fruits on the bountiful trees,
"Why, mortals, destroy us, brute passions to feed?
Is the chief end of fruitage the drunkard to please?
Is the grape yet to grow for the wine-seller's greed?"

"Do the sun, air, and rain come to earth in their wrath?
Does God till the ground for a vintage of blood?
Is the demon of hatred in every path?
Lurks the spirit of murder in every flood?"

"No! no!" saith a voice from the infinite space,
Encircling the earth, an omnipotent train;
"Love, peace, and good-will for the whole human race!
Our God, our Creator, makes nothing in vain!

"'Tis man, guilty man! in his passion and pride,
Who poisons the fountain of life at its flow!
A drunkard engulfed in the merciless tide,
He is sinking, by millions, to ruin and woe!"

REV. CHARLES WHEELER DENISON.

THE REFORM WILL GO ON.

INTEMPERANCE is not a mere local affair, but strikes at the very vitals of the nation. The liquor traffic is the fruitful source of woe, crime, misery, taxation, pauperism, and death.

Bear me witness if I exaggerate when I say that the country is rapidly becoming one vast grog-shop, to which half a million of its youth are yearly introduced, and over whose threshold sixty thousand are annually carted to a drunkard's grave. The streets of our cities echo to the shouts and oaths of drunken revellers, from whom society seeks protection through police regulations; and within hovel and mansion alike, not entirely smothered either by physical fear or social pride, is heard the sound of insane violence and wailing.

There are some who say the temperance movement is a sentimental affair, and that the reform will not go on. The reform will go on. Point me to a reform which ever stopped. Why, reform is motion, and motion ceaselessly acted upon by the impulse of acceleration; so is it with the temperance movement. From whatever standpoint you look at it, it is seen to be in exact harmony with the age; nay, it is a part of the age itself. The great civil revolution is to be supplemented with a great social revolution. God has so written it down. He has blessed the efforts of its friends until it has already taken a strong hold on the popular heart. Its champions are not fanatics; they are not sentimentalists; only terribly in earnest. Back of them are memories which will not let them pause. Broken circles and ruined altars, and fallen roof-trees, and the cold, sodden ashes of once genial fires, urge them on. No fear such men and women will falter, until you can take out of the human mind painful recollection; until you can make the children forget the follies and vices of the parents, over which they mounted to usefulness and to honor; until the memory will surrender from its custody the oaths of drunken blasphemy and the pains of brutal violence; until you can do these things, no man, no combination of men, can stop this reform. Its cause lies deep as human feeling itself. It draws its current from sources embedded in the very fastnesses of man's nature. The reform, then, will *go on.* It will go on because its principles are correct and its progress beneficent. The wave which has been gathering force and volume for these fifty years will continue to roll, because the hand of the Lord is under and back of it, and the denunciations of its opponents, and the bribed eloquence of the unprincipled, cannot check, no, nor retard, the onward movement of its flow. Upon the white crest of it thousands will be lifted to virtue and honor, and thousands more who put themselves in front of it will be submerged and swept away. The crisis through which this reform is passing will do good. It will make known its friends, and unmask its foes. The concussions above and around us will purify the atmosphere; and when the clouds have parted and melted away, we shall breathe purer air and behold sunnier skies.

We know not, indeed, what is ahead; what desertion of apparent friends may occur; what temporary defeat we may have to bear; nor against what intrigues we may be called upon to guard. For one, I count on the opposition of parties. I anticipate the double-dealing of political leaders. The cause more than once may be betrayed into the hands of its foes; more than once be deserted by those who owe to it whatever of prominence they have. But these reflections do not move me. They stir no ripple of fear on the surface of my hope. No good cause can ever be lost by the faithlessness of the unfaithful; no true principle of government overthrown by the opposition of its enemies; nor the progress of any reform, sanctioned by God and promotive of human weal, long retarded by any force or combination which can be marshalled against it. Over throne and proud empires the Gospel has marched, treading bayonets, and banners, and emblems of royalty proudly under its feet; and out of that Gospel no principle or tendency essential to the kingdom that is yet to be established on the earth can be selected so weak or so repugnant to fallen men as not to receive, ere the coming of that kingdom, its triumphant vindication. On this rock I plant my feet, and from its elevation contemplate the future, as a traveller gazes upon a landscape waving in golden-headed fruitfulness underneath the azure of a cloudless sky.

The Rain-Drops.

A FARMER had a field of corn of rather large extent,
In tending which, with anxious care, much time and toil he spent;
But after working long and hard, he saw, with grief and pain,
His corn began to droop and fade, because it wanted rain.

So sad and restless was his mind, at home he could not stop,
But to his field repaired each day to view his withering crop.
One day, when he stood looking up, despairing, at the sky,
Two little rain-drops in the clouds his sad face chanced to spy.

"I very sorry feel," said one, "to see him look so sad;
I wish I could do him some good; indeed, I should
be glad.
Just see the trouble he has had; and if it should not
rain,
Why, all his toil, and time, and care he will have
spent in vain."

"What use are you," cried number two, "to water
so much ground?
You're nothing but a drop of rain, and could not
wet one mound."
"What you have said," his friend replied, "I know
is very true;
But I'm resolved to do my best, and more I cannot do.

I'll try to cheer his heart a bit; so now I'm off—here
goes!"
And down the little rain-drop fell upon the farmer's
nose.
"Whatever's that?" the farmer cried. "Was it a drop
of rain?
I do believe it's come at last; I have not watched in
vain."

Now, when the second rain-drop saw his willing friend
depart,
Said he, "I'll go as well, and try to cheer the farmer's
heart."
But many rain-drops by this time had been attracted out,
To see and hear what their two friends were talking
so about.

"We'll go as well," a number cried, "as our two friends
have gone.
We shall not only cheer his heart, but water, too, his
corn.

We're off! we're off!" they shout with glee, and down they fell so fast.
"O bless the Lord!" the farmer cried, "the rain has come at last."

The corn it grew and ripened well, and into food was dressed,
Because a little rain-drop said, "I'll try, and do my best."
This little lesson, children dear, you'll not forget I'm sure;
Try, do your best, do what you can—angels can do no more.

T. H. EVANS.

GOING DOWN-HILL.

A STORY they tell of a lunatic man,
Who slid down-hill on a warming-pan,
He steered himself with the handle, of course
And checked away as he would to a horse.

His legs, it is true, were somewhat in the way,
And his seat rather tight, if a body might say;
But he landed all right at the foot of the hill,
And, for all that I know, he is sitting there still.

You smile at the story, and wonder how folks
Can get from their brains such a terrible hoax;
But sliding down-hill is many a man
On a much worse thing than a warming-pan.

Some are going down at full speed on their pride,
And others who on their stinginess slide;
But the strangest way of taking that ride
Is to go, as some do, on a beer-jug astride.

Beware of such coasting, or, like Jack and Gill,
You'll make sorry work in getting down-hill;
Beware! for, with what other evil you tug,
'Tis nothing like sliding down-hill on a jug.

OUR WARFARE.

STILL the fight goes on. The conflict is fearful. The rum army destroys; the temperance army saves. We have a desperate enemy to resist. It has millions of capital invested, hundreds of thousands of men enlisted; greed and still baser passions impel them onward. There are not less than 300,000 retail liquor-sellers, using every cunning artifice to secure customers. They are indefatigable home missionaries of the rum power. They are priests in the church of sin. They hold protracted meetings week after week, year after year, without cessation. They have hosts of recruiting agents, who compel men to come in; they push their work with ceaseless energy. Their power over their victims is wonderful. Once in their grasp, escape is the exception. Step by step they lead to certain ruin. And those who are most certain of ruin are always the least alarmed. They fear no evil, will not believe themselves in danger, and so go blindly to destruction. Every victim becomes a decoy to others. The youth especially seem ambitious to be ensnared. Hence converts are easily made.

Do any expect to cure this evil speedily? It cannot be done. The war will be long and hard. The enemy has capital, greed, appetite, all the powers of depravity, on his side. He concentrates every element of sin in his support; he embodies the aggregate powers of Satan. We might as well face the fact and know the worst. Our task is a hard one. Intemperance is a black cancer on the body of civilization. It will cost a terrible struggle to remove it.

But it must be done. The hope of the Gospel, of everything good, depends upon it. If Christianity cannot eradicate this enemy, it will strangle Christianity. It is not papacy, nor infidelity, nor worldliness that we have most to fear. These are not the greatest enemies to religion. Intemperance is the giant foe. It is the chief obstacle to the salvation of men. The great question now is, Who shall reign, Christ or rum?

If we are to resist sin at all, we must resist the liquor traffic. If we are sent to save the lost, we must rescue young men from tippling habits. The whole power of the churches, the influence of the Sabbath-schools, the testimony of the pulpits, must be emphatically against every form and degree of indulgence of this character. We must increase our opposition more and more; we should make it a leading point, so that social, commercial, and political action will be controlled by it; so that our preaching, praying, singing, talking, and voting will be full of it. The issue is radical, and requires energetic treatment. The victory of rum means return to barbarism; its defeat means Christian civilization. We must do our duty valiantly, at whatever cost.

BAPTIST UNION.

Mind the Door.

From mind the door, these little words,
  So often fraught with meaning,
We all may, whether young or old,
  Be useful lessons gleaning.

Now, there are various kinds of doors,
  To suit the purpose needed:
Both iron doors and wooden doors,
  And other kinds unheeded.

More choice the prize, more strong the door.
  For instance, see the bankers
Trust to their doors with bolts and bars,
  As sailors do to anchors.

We each have got two doors to mind,
  However we may do it;
And we must always seek the good,
  Flee evil and eschew it.

There's first the door of our own heart,
  With every evil reeking;
And next the door of our own lips,
  To keep from evil speaking.

And mind not only what comes out,
  But also what goes in them;
And never put the demon's drink,
  At any time between them.

For if you do, the danger's great
  Of falling into ruin;
And if you do in them indulge,
  'Twill be your soul's undoing,

And if you take those cursed drinks—
  Ale, wine, rum, gin, or brandy—
They bring home all the evil fruits
  That Satan keeps so handy.

So we'll make strong the outward door
  By totally abstaining;
And also keep the inner door
  By careful watch and training.

A Model Temperance Speech.

I PROPOSE to consider the temperance cause.
How it has run,
What it has done,
Where it is known,
What is its tone,
Why it has flourished,
How it is nourished.

1. How has it run?
It has run steadily,
It has run merrily.

2. What has it done?
It has 'rested the mad,
Reformed the bad,
Refreshed the sad,
Improved the glad.
It has cooled many a lip,
It has saved many a ship.

3. Where is it known?
In every zone.

4. What is its tone?
Its tone is inviting,
Its tone is delighting.

Look at the youthful Band of Hope. See how the children flock in crowds. See how happy they are. See what delight they give to their parents. See the happy families it makes. See the reformed drunkard's wife as her husband in his right mind comes home. See his happy children as they go to Sunday-school, and the happy change in himself.

5. Why has it flourished?
Because it is nourished.

6. How is it nourished?
By lectures and orations,
By books and illustrations,
By subscriptions and donations,
By glorious expectations.

Now, gentlemen, please bring forward the pledge, and pass round the plate.

The Decanter and the Dram-Shop.

I would have every minister of Christ put temperance where God puts it—in his heart and in the daily activities and perils of life. If into that door faithful preaching brings a soul to Christ, and at that rear door the bottle tempts another soul to ruin, what right has the pulpit to preach to that door, and turn its back upon the other? To-day the decanter and the dram-shop are sending more souls to perdition than all our pulpits are saving with the blessing of God upon their efforts!

Think a moment of that. The decanter and the dram-shop are ruining more homes and more hearts, and destroying more souls, than all our pulpits and Sabbath-schools are saving. And yet we meet many men who tell us that this is a question outside of the church, the ministry, the Sabbath-school, and the prayer-meeting. Let some of you tell me how often in your social prayer-meeting you hear prayer made for the drunkard, or for the salvation of our boys from the bottle and the drunkard's doom. People pray for China and the islands of the sea, for the overthrow of superstition and the casting down of heathenism, and this is all right; but silent is their lip towards God in reference to that insatiate demon that is bearing away one hundred thousand souls into a drunkard's grave every year. If you will tell me how often this great question is brought forward in social prayer-meetings, monthly concerts, Sabbath-schools, and churches, I will tell you how stands the temperance tide in that Christian community. We have got to dig deeper and go more thoroughly to the roots of things than by mere resolutions and conventions and the formation of parties on paper. Every one of us will have to take this question before God on our knees, as a lover of his country and of his kind, and ask him to give us courage, wisdom, tenderness, and power to do our part in the great question of the hour.

REV. T. L. CUYLER.

"STAND TO YOUR GUNS."

HOIST your flag! tis the eve of a fight
For the death of the demon of drink;
Draw your swords in the cause of the right!
Souls are loitering over the brink

Of a precipice, gloomy and dark,
  Whose base is the kingdom of hell;
So brace up your nerves for the fray,
  See to it you bear yourselves well.
        "Stand to your guns!"

Keep in line, for the foemen are strong;
  In numbers they rival the stars.
For the rescue of brothers from death,
  On to victory, and heed not your scars!
For the sake of the wives of your hearts,
  For the sake of the sisters you love,
For your babes, for your homes, for your all,
  Stand you fast—from your ranks do not move.
        "Stand to your guns!"

Fire away! till the haunts of the fiend—
  Those poison-shops, gates to the grave—
Shall be levelled to earth by your shot;
  Hurl them down, not a stone of them save!
For the blood of the slain stains their walls,
  The souls of the lost cry, "Repay!"
The maniac's laugh and the idiot's smile
  Command you to sweep them away.
        "Stand to your guns!"

Look to God! for he only can help,
  And he loveth the banner you bear;
Do not fear, hold it bravely aloft,
  Seek the thick of the fight—be you there!
Live in hope, do not tremble or faint,
  If the battle be weary and long;
Dash forward! redouble your blows!
  And, till victory tuneth your song,
        "Stand to your guns!"

HENRY ANDERTON.

JACK SIMPSON'S DREAM.

JACK SIMPSON was a reckless chap,
His best friends said he'd come to ruin;
But then, it mattered not a rap,
He never cared what he was doing.

One night, when drunk, he rambled on,
Down street and lane, till near a river
He stood, and thought himself to drown
And thus his mad career to sever.

The night was dark, no moon appeared,
No sound was heard save wild winds playing,
Thoughts wiser came—the end he feared;
When, lo! he heard a donkey braying.

And yet it was a startling sound,
It seemed with terror to assail him;
He thought himself on hallowed ground,
Where spake the very ass of Balaam.

Jack silent stood. The ass thus spake:
"Leap, wretch, into this gliding river'
Better thy grave with fishes make
Than be an idle, drunken liver.

"I am an ass, but thou a man
With soul endued and powers increasing,
Destined God's wondrous works to scan,
And be to all thy race a blessing.

"I am an ass of meanest worth,
With instinct only like another;
Yet I fulfil my part on earth,
And would not own *thee* as a brother.

"Thou art an idle, drunken pest,
The centre of a thousand evils—
A reckless sinner at the best,
And only fit to dwell with devils."

At this last word there seemed to rise
The very flames of hell around him,
And imps of hideous form and size,
And devils, came with chains and bound him.

Away like lightning then they flew,
And bore him to the place of demons.
"Mercy!" he cried, "can this be true,
Or do I feel *delirium tremens?*"

The sun had risen in the east
When he awoke to sense and feeling;
"Save, Lord!" he cried, and smote his breast,
And angels saw a sinner kneeling.

That dream he ne'er is wont to tell,
So terrible and so appalling;
Each day he thinks of death and hell,
And prays for grace to keep from falling.

The very gates of hell he sees
In every drinking-shop and tavern;
And from their portals now he flees
As from a pestilential cavern.

Give Me Back My Husband.

NOT many years since, a young married couple from the far "fast-anchored isle" sought our shores with the most sanguine anticipations of happiness and prosperity. They had begun to realize more than they had seen in the visions of hope, when, in an evil hour, the husband was tempted "to look upon the wine when it is red," and to taste of it "when it giveth its color in the cup." The charmer fastened round its victim all the serpent-spells of its sorcery, and he fell; and at every step of his degradation from the man to the brute, and downward, a heart-string broke in the bosom of his companion.

Finally, with the last spark of hope flickering on the altar of her heart, she threaded her way into one of those shambles where man is made such a thing as the beasts of the field would bellow at. She pressed her way through the bacchanalian crowd who were revelling there in their own ruin. With her bosom full of "that perilous stuff that preys upon the heart," she stood before the plunderer of her husband's destiny, and exclaimed in tones of startling anguish, "*Give me back my husband!*"

"There's your husband," said the man, as he pointed toward the prostrate wretch.

"*That my husband?* What have you done to him? *That my husband?* What have you done to that noble form that once, like the great oak, held its protecting shade over the fragile vine that clung to it for support and shelter? *That my husband?* With what torpedo chill have you touched the sinews of that manly arm? What have you done to that once noble brow, which he wore high among his fellows, as if it bore the superscription of the Godhead? *That my husband?* What have you done to that eye, with which he was wont to look erect on heaven, and see in his mirror the image of his God? What Egyptian drug have you poured into his veins, and turned the ambling fountains of the heart into black and burning pitch? Give me back my husband! Undo your basilisk spells, and give me back the *man* that stood with me by the altar!"

The ears of the rumseller, ever since the first demijohn of that burning liquid was opened upon our shores, have been saluted, at every stage of the traffic, with just such appeals as this. Such wives, such widows, and mothers, such fatherless children, as never mourned in Israel at the massacre of Bethlehem or at the burning of the temple, have cried in his ears, morning, night, and evening, "*Give me back my husband! Give me back my boy! Give me back my brother!*"

But has the rumseller been confounded or speechless at these appeals? No! not he. He could show his credentials at a moment's notice with proud defiance. He always carried in his pocket a written absolution for all he had done and could do in his work of destruction. *He had bought a letter of indulgence*—I mean a *license!*—a precious instrument, signed and sealed by an authority stronger and more respectable than the pope's. *He* confounded? Why, the whole artillery of civil power was ready to open in his defence and support. Thus shielded by the law, he had nothing to fear from the enemies of his traffic. He had the image and superscription of Cæsar on his credentials, and unto Cæsar he appealed; and unto Cæsar, too, his *victims* appealed, and *appealed in vain.*

ONLY SIXTEEN.

"When last seen, he was considerably intoxicated, . . . and was found dead in the highway."—*Republican and Democrat* of May 17.

ONLY sixteen, so the papers say,
Yet there on the cold, stony ground he lay;
'Tis the same sad story we hear every day—
He came to his death in the public highway.
Full of promise, talent, and pride,
Yet the rum fiend conquered him; so he died.
Did not the angels weep over the scene?
For he died a drunkard—and only sixteen,
Only sixteen.

Oh! it were sad he must die all alone;
That of all his friends, not even one
Was there to list to his last faint moan,
Or point the suffering soul to the throne
Of grace. If, perchance, God's only Son
Would say, "Whosoever will may come."
But we hasten to draw a veil over the scene,
With his God we leave him—only sixteen,
Only sixteen.

Rumseller, come view the work you have wrought;
Witness the suffering and pain you have brought
To the poor boy's friends. They loved him well,
And yet you dared the vile beverage to sell
That beclouded his brain, his reason dethroned,
And left him to die out there all alone.
What if 'twere *your* son instead of another?
What if your wife were that poor boy's mother,
And he only sixteen?

Ye free-holders who signed the petition to grant
The license to sell, do you think you will want
That record to meet in the last great day,
When the earth and the heavens shall have passed away,
When the elements, melting with fervent heat,
Shall proclaim the triumph of RIGHT complete?
Will you wish to have his blood on your hands
When before the great throne you each shall stand,
And he only sixteen?

Christian men! rouse ye to stand for the right,
To action and duty; into the light
Come with your banners, inscribed "Death to rum."
Let your conscience speak. Listen, then, come;

Strike killing blows; hew to the line;
Make it a felony even to sign
A petitiōn to license; you would do it, I ween,
If that were your son, and "only sixteen,"
Only sixteen.

THE WATCHWORD.

THE SCOLDING OLD DAME.

THERE once was a toper—I'll not tell his name—
Who had for his comfort a scolding old dame;
And often and often he wished himself dead,
For, if drunk he came home, she would beat him to bed.
He spent all his evenings away from his home,
And, when he returned, he would sneakingly come
And try to walk straightly, and say not a word—
Just to keep his dear wife from abusing her lord;
For if he dared say his tongue was his own,
'Twould set her tongue going, in no gentle tone,
And she'd huff him, and cuff him, and call him hard names,
And he'd sigh to be rid of all scolding old dames.

It happened, one night, on a frolic he went,
He stayed till his very last penny was spent;
But how to go home, and get safely to bed,
Was the thing on his heart that most heavily weighed.
But home he must go; so he caught up his hat,
And off he went singing, by this and by that,
"I'll pluck up my courage; I guess she's in bed.
If she an't, 'tis no matter, I'm sure. Who's afraid?"
He came to his door; he lingered until
He peeped, and he listened, and all seemed quite still,
In he went, and his wife, sure enough, was in bed!
"Oh!" says he, "it's just as I thought. Who's afraid?"

He crept about softly, and spoke not a word;
His wife seemed to sleep, for she never e'en stirred!
Thought he, "For *this* night, then, my fortune is made;
For my dear, scolding wife is asleep! Who's afraid?"
But soon he felt thirsty; and slyly he rose,
And, groping around, to the table he goes,
The pitcher found empty, and so was the bowl,
The pail, and the tumblers—she'd emptied the whole!
At length, in a corner, a vessel he found!
Says he, "Here's something to drink, I'll be bound!"
And eagerly seizing, he lifted it up—
And drank it all off in one long, hearty sup!

It tasted so queerly; and what could it be?
He wondered. It neither was water nor tea!
Just then a thought struck him and filled him with fear:
"Oh! it must be the poison for rats, I declare!"
And loudly he called on his dear, sleeping wife,
And begged her to rise; "for," said he, "on my life
I fear it was *poison* the bowl did contain.
Oh dear! yes, it *was* poison; I now feel the pain!"
"And what made you dry, sir?" the wife sharply cried.
"'Twould serve you just right if from poison you died;
And you've done a *fine* job, and you'd now better march,
For just see, you brute, you have drunk all my starch!"

PROHIBITION.

WHAT is meant by prohibition? We do not intend by prohibition to enact a bill of fare for the people. We do not propose any sumptuary measures for the regulation of mankind. We do not design to give directions by legislative enactments to physicians in relation to the dietetic treatment of their patients. We simply ask for a law which shall be lifted as a shield to save our fellow-men from the terrible blow which is aimed at them by the liquor traffic. We ask the men who make our laws to protect us from the evils which accompany the rum trade. The rum trade makes men mad, and under the influence of rum men will assault their neighbors, starve and beat their wives and children, commit theft, arson, and murder. We ask men of every shade of politics, of every creed in religion, to join with us in our earnest efforts to stop the liquor traffic and seal up the dram-shops. Is it unreasonable and arbitrary to demand a law which shall squelch the cause of the effect we all deplore. Here is a man who contributes nothing toward his own support; he is a tax and a nuisance, vibrating between the grog-shop and the station-house. Sober men have to foot his bills, support his family, suffer the infliction of his bad habits, and run the risk of his torch and his knife. Now is this a fair and square condition of things? Shall the innocent be burdened with the sins of the guilty? That man would take care of himself and of those who depend upon him, if the liquor-shops were closed. He would contribute his share of tax toward the support of the institutions of government, and he would cease to be a scarecrow in society. Now rum lights his torch; rum nerves his arm to strike the innocent; rum fires the temper which makes his mouth break out in eruptions of wicked speech; rum sharpens the blade of assassination. We ask for a law of prohibition which shall say, without circumlocution, "No man shall poison another man; no man shall sell to another that which will deprive his mind of reason and his heart of feeling." We demand prohibition because it is in accordance with the laws of self-preservation—the first law of nature; because it is practical, and has worked wonders of reform where it has been carried into execution; because the tax-payers and all the decent members of society, and the wives and children of all, are entitled to its protection; because even the dram-sellers and their drunken victims will be benefited by it; and because it is in unison with the high and holy enactments of God in the Ten Commandments. There we find no half-way law, no license for the committing of sin. "Thou shalt not steal," is the language of the Scriptures. He who receives money without returning an equivalent steals. The rumseller does not give an equivalent for the money he receives; hence he steals. We ask our human legislators to echo the divine legislation, and say to the dealers in rum, "Thou shalt not steal." Thou shalt not make thy neighbor steal. "Thou shalt not kill" by selling that which does kill a hundred thousand victims a year. Prohibition is the translation of the sixth commandment into human law, "Thou shalt not kill"—not even for five hundred, or five thousand dollars a year. "Thou shalt not kill" with arsenic, nor with alcohol, by degrees nor suddenly, in the city nor in the country. This is prohibition. We want to prohibit vice and crime, theft and murder, and all the evils which flow from intemperance.

R. C. PITMAN.

THE MODERN GOLIATH—ALCOHOL.

"And David said, What have I now done? Is there not a cause?"—I. Sam. xvii. 29.

FULL forty days Philistia's host defiant
  By Elah's vale filled Israel with dismay,
As, overawed by Gath's ungainly giant,
  Saul and the Hebrew bands all trembling lay.
A shepherd "stripling" heard the challenge flaunted,
  And straight with holy indignation stung,
At grim Goliath's haughty mien undaunted,
  Back on the scornful foe defiance flung;

And meekly, ere to that dread strife he draws,
His brother's taunt he answers: "*Is there not a cause?*"

A giant demon now abroad is walking,
Who frowns defiance on the Christian host;
And whilst before their ranks that foe is stalking,
Alas! of dire destruction he can boast.
Say, ye who serve your Lord and love his laws,
For deeds of faith and venture "*Is there not a cause?*"

What if for comrades' fall your eyes be tearful?
The weak against the strong can still prevail.
If other hearts of this assault be fearful,
No warrior of Christ should ever quail.
Not seeking human aid or man's applause
To arm him for the fray: he knows *there is a cause.*

Great Captain, thou thine own hast not forsaken,
But with our host still goest forth to fight;
Our languid faith revive, our soul awaken,
Thou Lord of power and Giver of all might;
While from the field each craven heart withdraws,
That we, like men should quit us: "Is there not a cause?"

DRINKING DOES NOT PAY!

GO with me to every jail and prison throughout our land, from ocean to ocean, and ascertain how large a portion of those crimes and misdemeanors that have taken men from their families and lodged them there in prison walls has resulted from intoxication; and the answer from every jail and prison comes to us to-night that "drinking does not pay." Visit the poor-houses, which the charities of mankind provide for those who from competency have been reduced to destitution, and learn there the sad lesson, how many of them have ceased to become useful and valuable members of society, and dependent upon the taxes by which we support the poor, in consequence of yielding to the intoxicating bowl; and every poor-house answers, "Drinking does not pay." Examine the statistics of the gallows, and learn how many of its victims were induced to take the downward road thither by that intoxicating cup which turned their brains and nerved their arm for the blow which sent them to the gallows; and the gallows tells you that "drinking does not pay." Read history, and learn from it how many of the great and the gifted in other lands as well as our own have commenced at wine-drinking and ended in ruin, mental and physical; and history tells you that "drinking does not pay." Nay, more, read the papers of the day, and from every quarter you hear, morning after morning, and evening after evening, of the thousands who, once having pledged at the altar a lifetime of devotion and affection to their brides, reel home from a drunken debauch, to treat with brutality and violence those who should be as dear to them as their heart's blood; and this army of worse than widowed wives, whose woes no one but themselves can realize, tells you most sadly and impressively that "drinking does not pay."

It has been well said, "It is the first step that costs." Young men, stepping out upon the threshold of life, with everything bright and hopeful in your future, let me adjure you, above all things else next to devotion to that religion which is to smooth your pathway to the tomb, avoid taking that first step. Plant your feet upon that solid rock of sobriety, as well as of safety, and then you may know that, so far as intemperance is concerned, its waves can dash against you, but they will dash in vain.

HON. SCHUYLER COLFAX.

Opening Speech.

SHOULD you ask me whence these children,
Whence the young men and these maidens?
I should answer, I should tell you,
From the hills and valleys round us,
From the homes that proudly own them.
Should you ask me why the children,
Why the young men and these maidens,
Have thus gathered here together?
I should answer, I should tell you,
They have come to pledge their friendship
To the fountains and the streamlets,
To the clear, refreshing waters;
They would thrust for ever from them
All the liquors that are evil—
Sparkling wine, that old deceiver,
Deadly as the stinging adder,
With all hard and stupid cider,
And the strong and fiery brandy;
Punch and whiskey are included,
And the mug of sweetened toddy;
And they come to give the promise
That they will not ever utter
Oaths against their heavenly Father.
This is why have come the children
Singing songs of cheer and gladness;
Speaking words of joy and sadness;
That they may not join with drunkards,
Nor with swearers, nor with smokers,
But in all good ways may follow
Footsteps of the blessed Saviour,
And so please their heavenly Father.

Found Dead Drunk.

A PARODY.

ONE more inebriate
  Into the gutter.
"Thick-headed muddlepate,"
  Hear the crowd mutter.
Take him up roughly,
  Blue-coated star,
Shake him, and pitch gruffly
  Into the car.

Look at his hat so battered,
His face quite bespattered,
While the mud constantly
  Drips from his clothing.
Off with him instantly,
  Spurn him with loathing.

Touch him not mournfully,
Think of him scornfully,
  Treat him not humanly.
Beware the stains of him!
Into the lock-up with him.
  Let him sleep fumily.

Look at the blotches
  That bloom on his nose—
Glowing *red* blotches,
Scars, seams, and notches,
  As red as the rose.

Who is his father?
  Where is his mother?
Has he a brother?
  Or is there another
To keep this sot out of jail,
Will at once sign for his bail,
  And away with this bother?

Alas! for the rarity
Of Christian charity
  Under the sun!
Oh! it is pitiful!
In a whole cityful,
  Friend he has none.

Where the lamps quiver,
So far on the river,
  With bright, sparkling light
From window and casement,
From garret to basement,
We stand with amazement,
  And gaze at the sight.

That we now behold
  Makes us tremble and shiver.
Not with *piercing cold*
  Do we tremble and shiver—
Here, the life history,
This, the paupers' mystery,
  Is thus unfurled.
Yes, here! Ah! here:
  Cursed of the world.

In this gambling hell,
Rum poison they sell

To this miserable man.
'Tis death to drink it;
Pause o'er it, think of it,
Anti-temperance man.
Vote for it, drink of it
Then, if you can.

Snatch it away quickly,
Linger not there.
Young man, ever so strictly
Of wine-cups beware!

PHIL. O. SOPHER.

TEMPERANCE AND RELIGION.

TEMPERANCE is not religion, but it is one of the virtues of religion. A man may be a temperance man without being a religious man; but he cannot be a pious or religious man so long as he remains an intemperate man. Temperance is an aid of religion; the ally of Christianity, preparing the mind and heart to receive the truth of religion. It casts the devil of drunkenness out of the man; sweeps the temple of the soul with the pledge of abstinence, and fits it to receive the holy influence of true piety. There is no antagonism between temperance and religion, for the former prepares the way for the latter. Temperance societies are the nurseries of the church; temperance tracts are the leaves which are intended for the healing of the nations; temperance lectures are the voice of John the Baptist in the wilderness. Drunkenness is a physical disease, breaking out in blotches upon the face, and sapping and mining the foundations of health and life. The pledge is a panacea which never fails to cure the disease when it is taken in time and kept inviolate. Drunkenness is also a moral malady, and religion is the remedy which is sure to cure it when it is taken from the hand which offers it. Those men who trust to temperance for salvation are like the carpenters of Noah, who built a ship for other folks to sail in, and yet were drowned themselves at last.

Lulu's Speech.

I AM a little temperance girl
  Just five years old;
I wouldn't drink a glass of wine
  If you'd fill the cup with gold.
I have a little brother,
  We belong to the Band of Hope;
I 'spect there'll be no drunken men
  When he and I grow up.
For, don't you see, the *little ones*
  Are all going to join the Band,
And we'll soon be *great big temperance folks.*
  Oh! won't that be *so grand*
When there's not a drunkard to be seen?
  For, don't you think its queer,
The *first thing* drunkards learn to drink
  Is the *cider, wine, and beer!*
And so we belong to the Band of Hope,
  And we mean to be *good* and *true;*
And all the little boys and girls
  We shall ask to join us, too.

MRS. E. J. RICHMOND.

The Drunken Mother.

A TRUE STORY.

THE waning moon hung out her feeble light;
Dim stars shone here and there one winter night.
Amongst abodes of indigence and care,
Down a dark court, a wretched home stood there.

The house three stories high—the bottom floor
Saw squalid poverty unseen before;
No pestilence or famine cursed the land,
But o'er that house intemp'rance waved its wand.

The dying embers long had ceased to blaze
On hearth once bright with light of better days;
Intoxication with its fearful blast,
Like a destroying angel, had been past.

There lonely children sat with weary eyes,
'Twas near the Sabbath morning's peaceful rise;
The absent mother, so required within,
Was at the tavern drinking ale or gin.

They talked of her, told of their wants and woes—
How pledged their shoes, and from their backs the clothes;
How all the thoughts that ever she could think
Were sacrificed unto her idol—Drink.

The spirit-bottle on the secret shelf
Ruined her home, her children, and herself;
Affection, pity, anger—all in vain;
Oft she repented, and then drank again.

And strongly urged by kindness to abstain,
She said she would, and never drink again;
She signed the pledge, but soon that vow was broke,
And then the demon Drink confirmed his yoke.

The circling ball rolls on when once begun—
Thus good and evil must their courses run.
One night, with indistinctive thoughts of bed,
She reeled home dizzy, stumbled, and was dead.

The extra glass to bid a friend good-by
Was the first cloud that darkened all their sky,
And those whom once she fondly called her own
Through insatiate thirst on Providence were thrown.

The fairest flower of Eden still bears seed—
Man's joy in sorrow and his help in need;
But she made life and prospect here below
"A mourning, lamentation, and a woe."

This moral learn: to grow to hardened sin,
We only need by littles to begin;
And then, when hope of reformation's past,
A long-forbearing judgment comes at last.

CHARLES CROSS.

LOOK NOT ON THE WINE WHEN IT IS RED.

BEWARE! oh! beware!
Young stranger, take care,
When it sparkles before thee so brilliant and fair;
And away turn thine eye
To yon pure azure sky,
And think of his word who is Sovereign there.

Though at first it delight thee,
Like a serpent 'twill bite thee,
And sting like an adder! Beware! oh! beware!
If the wine-cup be bright,
'Tis a treacherous light,
And will lead thee to ruin. Oh! flee from the snare!

Cold Water Greeting.

I AM glad to be here to-night. Here we are assembled in the name of God, who has taken care of us all our lives long, who has sent his Son to redeem us, and who has sent his Holy Spirit to cleanse us. We began this meeting with a prayer, and we will close it with a benediction. Let heaven rejoice, and hell tremble; let all the grog-shops from Nova Scotia to California hallo; we will set up our banners. I cannot understand why all the poets and romancers, when they begin to talk about a good time, always gather it around a wine-bottle or ale-cask, as if people could not have a good time unless they became half drunk. I don't believe there is a man here who has taken anything stronger than Hyson tea or Old Dominion coffee; and have you ever seen a merrier group? Cold water is good for the constitution. It puts no gout into the toes; it puts no dimness into the eyes; it puts no trembling into the limbs. It never sets a man at midnight interviewing a lamp-post. It never turns respectable men into gutter inspectors. It never turns domestic arrangements upside down until the father is as bad off as the man who said that none of his children took after him, except his eldest daughter, and she took after him with a broomstick. I read in some paper a very learned disquisition showing that alcohol is just the thing for the constitution, especially for those with the *medulla oblongata*, or something like that, which I suppose to be something similar to the disease with which Mrs. Brent was afflicted. Her husband was a very illiterate man; he thought he would not have a doctor, and that he would read up and treat the case himself. He afterward told a friend that he believed his wife was threatened with a very bad attack of "diagnosis," and that, if she got that, she would be a "goner." And true enough, in a very few weeks, it was inscribed on her tombstone:

"Here lies Mrs. Brent;
She kicked up her heels, and away she went."

I think that cold water is not only good for the body, but it keeps us, as we are all found to-night, in good heart and at peace with all the world; and, taking the words of the only out-and-out temperance man who ever lived in the White House, "We have malice toward none, and charity for all."

For those poor fellows who are the victims of strong drink we have compassion, we have prayer, we have Christian sympathy, we have all help. For those who sell rum we have deep pity that they should bring upon themselves the scorn of good society; that they should bring upon themselves the retributions of eternity.

When a man comes with a soul and body all on fire with evil habits, and looks up into the face of the Lord God, and says, "Help, help," I tell you that all the resources of omnipotence and eternity are pledged to that man's deliverance, and he will get it. Let us, as we start a new year form the resolution to do more work in the temperance cause. You who have pens, write; you who have tongues, speak; you who have helping hands, help. And God grant that there may be hundreds and hundreds of prodigals, with their scarred and palsied tongues looking heavenward, by our prayers and by our efforts brought out from their bondage.

"There's a labor to be wrought,
There's a race that we must run,
There's a battle to be fought,
And a victory to be won.
For a cheated nation's sake!
Ho, ye people! plundered all
By the slaves of alcohol,
Rouse, the demon's arm to break;
Wide awake, boys! wide awake."

REV. T. DE WITT TALMAGE.

THE DRUNKARD.

GIVE me drink, the drunkard said,
I will not take the temperance vow
Too long this dark'ning life I've led
For you to try to save me now;
And I could not, with my mad brain,
Share of the joys of life again.
Too many evils clasp my heart
For me to rend the bonds apart;
For me to try to see the dawn,
That breaks beyond the gloomy river,
When the soul from earth has gone
Back unto the Eternal Giver,
Disgraced and lost for evermore.
I shall not walk the sun-bright plain;
And it is useless to deplore
That which I cannot have again.
There was a time when I could claim,
Away back in the by-gone years,
A happy heart and honored name;
I then had no for boding fears,

And all the world was full of light,
And life to me was dear and bright.
But in the tempting glass I found
The demon that my soul has bound—
The demon that has led me on
From crime to crime, through sin and gloom,
Till every joy I loved is gone,
And I must meet a fearful doom,
And nevermore can hope to hear
Fond words from love-lips kindly spoken;
But must await in doubt and fear,
Until the last frail link is broken.
Yon pompous man now riding by,
With trotting bays and carriage fine,
Who never gives one pitying sigh,
First gave to me the tempting wine.
My earnings helped to place him there,
But now I cannot ride with him—
I'm lower than his classes are,
And my eyes are red and dim.
Will he be punished less than I
In the great eternity?
He took my hard-earned gold away,
And made me what I am to-day.
Poor Mary wept and prayed for me,
And, broken-hearted, died at last;
Her grave is down beside the sea,
And I can only mourn the past;
Can only in my grief await
The coming of a darker fate.
God knows I did not wish to be
The wretched being I am now;
The serpent clinging fast to me,
And shame and sin stamped on my brow,
And in my heart a pall of gloom
That dark and fatal makes my doom.

OLIVER PERRY MANLOVE.

FACTS WORTH KNOWING.

THERE is no greater evil in all Christendom than intemperance. There are no sterner reasons for any reform in the world than for the temperance reform. There is no evil producing such dreadful results; there is no cause that can be espoused in behalf of which so much can be said in its favor, so much in the way of fact and statistic and argument appealing to the mind. You have heard say that one hundred thousand lives are lost by intemperance. That may be a high estimate; they used to talk about sixty thousand as being the number of deaths occasioned by liquor. Sixty thousand annually destroyed! Have you any idea of what that means? Suppose that an earthquake should have swallowed up four cities like Auburn in this State; that would have made sixty thousand. Suppose another earthquake should swallow up another city in Pennsylvania, then another in some other State, and so it should go on year after year; how long would we be living in this land? Would we not leave it as we would fly from the pestilence? And yet sixty thousand lives are destroyed every year by alcoholic drinks. You have heard of the terrible accident that occurred on the Hudson River Railroad, when the express-train ran into an oil-train, and twenty lives were lost. As the morning paper was taken up, horror ran through the community; everybody felt thrilled with excitement in view of the awful havoc in connection with that railroad accident. Suppose that the next month a similar telegraphic dispatch was sent that another accident had happened on the same road, and next month another, throughout the year; that would have amounted to about two hundred and fifty lives lost on the Hudson River Railroad for a year. By the end of the year, there is not a man or woman in this city, who, if they heard of a friend of theirs talking about going to Albany on the Hudson River Railroad, but would go to that person, and endeavor, by all the influences they could command, to persuade that individual to keep off that road. Suppose these accidents occurred every week instead of monthly, or every day instead of every week, then you would have only seven thousand lives lost annually on that road, if tidings had come to you every morning of an accident of a similar nature. And then what would have been done? Why, that railroad would have been torn up from its base, the iron would have been pitched into the river, the ties would have been destroyed, and the cars burned to pieces, and this community would have said, "No more cars on that road." Suppose from eight other roads the same tidings had come, there would not be a railroad in the country, for no man would venture upon a car. If there were eight such accidents from eight different roads every day in the year, there would not be so many lives lost as are destroyed by intemperance. Now, these are facts; and facts like these need to be brought before the community, in order to inform the mind, touch the conscience, and arouse the heart.

REV. HERRICK JOHNSON.

THE LITTLE ARMIES.

THERE are two little armies
  On the world's great battle-field,
Though unnoted oft by mortals,
  To the eyes of God revealed.

Though we hear no shouts of triumph,
  Though we see no fearful fray,
Those little armies battle
  For the Right or Wrong each day;
  The Right or Wrong each day.

They *must fight;* no ground is neutral;
  And I watch the sides they take;
One little army chooses
  To fight for Truth's dear sake;
The banner floating o'er it
  Rises grandly up to view;
And I read this glorious motto:
  "Fighting for the Good and True;
  For Temperance and God."

How brave that little army!
  What a halo o'er it shines!
And even angels welcome
  Every soldier to its lines;
How sweet the stirring music
  Of the tramp of little feet
That in God's holy highway
  Swiftly onward, upward beat:
  Onward and upward beat.

Alas! the other army,
  'Neath a gloomy flag unfurled,
Marches with the ranks of evil;
  Treads the dark ways of the world;
Not for the true and beautiful
  Does it grow brave and strong;
For, lo! upon its banner
  I read, "Fighting for the Wrong;
  Old surly-hearted Wrong."

MARY FLETCHER BEAVERS.

An Acrostic on the Word Distillery.

DRINK naught that's made within my walls, list to my warning voice:
I deal in strongest poisons here, just watered to men's choice.
Save all your money, laboring men, and then you'll wisely see
'Twere better far to burn it all than take strong drink from me.
I and my masters are the cause of every drunkard's woe;
Leave off this dangerous trifling, then, which hurts your body so.
Look all around, and see the ills which spots like me have wrought;
Everywhere see my handiwork—give that your deepest thought.
Resolve without delay, and then, if from my path you look,
You'll live to bless the very day that my advice you took.

The Temperance Enterprise.

"AN enterprise that has fed the hungry, and clothed the naked, and healed the sick, and taught the ignorant, and elevated the degraded, and gladdened the sorrowful, and led to the cross multitudes that had been wandering far away; an enterprise that has gathered again the fortune that had been scattered, and built again the home that had been ruined, and raised again the character that had been blasted, and bound up the heart that had been broken; an enterprise that has given peace where there was discord, and gladness where there had been woe, that has broken open many a prison door, and restored to his right mind many a maniac; an enterprise that has prevented many a suicide, and that has robbed the gallows of many a victim that would otherwise have been there; an enterprise that has thinned the work-house, and the hospital, and the jail, but that has helped to fill the school, and the lecture-room, and the industrial exhibition; an enterprise that has turned into useful citizens those that were the pests of society, one of the best educators of the masses, one of the chief pioneers of the Gospel; an enterprise which is not Christ, but which is as one of the holy angels that go upon his mission. Like some fair spirit from another world, our great enterprise has trodden the wilderness, and flowers of beauty have sprung up upon her track. She has looked around, gladdening all on whom her smiles have fallen; she has touched the captive, and his fetters have fallen off; she has spoken, and the countenance of despair has been lighted up with hope; she has waved her magic wand, and the wilderness has rejoiced and blossomed as the rose. Like the fabled Orpheus, she has warbled her song of mercy, and wild beasts, losing their ferocity, have followed gladly and gratefully in her train. She has raised up those that have been worse than dead, sepulchred in sin, and she has led multitudes to the living waters of salvation."

NEWMAN HALL.

VOTE YES, OR NO.

VOTE yes, and the vile demon drink
  Shall raise its awful head on high,
That man, the noble work of God,
  May helpless in the gutter lie;

The drunkard's wife may starve and weep,
  And the poor children, all forlorn,
In their degraded sphere become
  Victims of drink and vice and scorn.

Vote no, and love and peace will dwell
  In the poor saved inebriate's home;
His wife will thank the God above
  Her husband never cares to roam;
The children, in their joyful glee,
  Have learnt to meet him with delight;
No more he drinks the drunkard's drink,
  Because you voted for the right.

Vote yes, and many an only son
  Will cause his mother's heart to ache,
For she with bitter sorrow finds
  His promises are made to break;
His craving appetite demands,
  And drink, he feels, must be supplied;
And so from paths of rectitude
  Helpless he wanders far and wide.

Vote no, and mothers good and true
  Will shower blessings on your head,
For many a son will be restored
  Whom drink a helpless victim led;
Drunkards will learn to walk erect,
  And many a home be filled with joy,
And many a son will be reformed,
  And many a mother bless her boy.

Vote yes, and paupers multiply,
  And crime of every sort will reign,
And man degraded will become
  A needless sufferer of pain;

Transformed, he will no longer seek
  To raise and help his fellow-man,
But to the deepest, darkest depths
  With bitter hate drag all he can.

Vote no, and He who made the world
  Will bless and crown the righteous deed;
Your prayers and votes with one accord
  Ask that the drunkard may be freed;
And God, the high, the just, and great,
  The double action will approve,
Because its promptings are sincere,
  The pure outgrowth of fervent love.

THOMAS R. THOMPSON.

SONG OF THE WATER.

YOU may find me in the mountain,
  In the little gurgling rills;
I am gushing from the fountain,
  And coursing down the hills.
I am rolling in the billows,
  And on the breakers ride;
My home is with the mariner
  Out on the ocean wide.

You may find me in the dew-drop
  That is glistening on the flowers;
I come to drooping nature
  In cool, refreshing showers.
I am glancing in the sunbeams
  From my cloud-spangled house on high,
And I come in dewy sadness,
  With tears that never dry.

You may find me in the river,
  Rushing on with ceaseless roar,
Until it meets its comrade
  By some far-off distant shore.
I am found in misty ether,
  Hanging, quivering o'er the earth,
And gathered up like pearl-drops,
  Ere the clouds have given me birth.

And I come in fleecy whiteness,
  Drifting, drifting lightly down,
Covering hill and vale and meadow
  With a pure and spotless gown—
An emblem of the beauty
  And the purity above,
Where the angels shine in glory
  In yonder world of love.

I bring health, and joy, and gladness
  Where'er I am used aright;
I sometimes chase the shadows,
  And make all faces bright.
Then fill each costly goblet,
  As you gather round the board,
With pure and sparkling water
  Brought from nature's choicest hoard.

A Drunken Soliloquy in a Coal-Cellar.

LET'S see, where am I? This is coal I'm lying on. How 'd I get here? Yes, I mind now; was coming up street; met a wheel-barrow what was drunk, coming t'other way. That wheel-barrow fell over me, or I fell over the wheel-barrow, and *one* of us fell into the cellar;

don't mind now which; guess it must have been me. I'm a nice young man; yes, I am—tight, tore, drunk, shot! Well, I can't help it, 'tan't my fault. Wonder whose fault it is? Is it Jones's fault? No! Is it my wife's fault? No-o-o! IT'S WHISKEY'S FAULT! WHISKEY! Who's whiskey? Has he got a large family? Got many relations? All poor, I reckon. I won't own him any more; cut his acquaintance I have had a notion of doing that for the last ten years; always hated to, though, for fear of hurting his feelin's. I'll do it now, for I believe liquor is injurin' me; it's spoilin' my temper. Sometimes I gets mad, and abuses Bets. When I come home, she used to put her arms around my neck and kiss me, and call me "dear William!" When I come home now, she takes her pipe out of her mouth, puts the hair out of her eyes, and looks at me and says, "Bill, you drunken brute, shut the door after you! We're cold enough, havin' no fire, 'thout lettin' the snow blow in that way." Yes, she's Bets, and I'm Bill now; I an't a good bill, nother; I'm counterfeit; won't pass (a tavern without goin' in and gettin' a drink). Don't know what bank I'm on; last Sunday was on the river-bank, at the Corn Exchange, drunk! I stay out pretty late—sometimes out all night, when Bets bars the door with a bed-post. Fact is, I'm out pretty much all over—out of friends, out of pocket, out at elbows and knees, and outrageously dirty. So Bets says; but she's no judge, for she's never clean herself. I wonder she don't wear good clothes. May be she an't got any! Whose fault is that? 'Tan't mine! It may be whiskey's. Sometimes I'm in; I'm in-toxicated now, and in somebody's coal-cellar. I've got one good principle: I never runs in debt—'cause nobody won't trust me. One of my coat-tails is gone; got tore off, I expect, when I fell down here. I'll have to get a new suit soon. A fellow told me t'other day that I'd make a good sign for a paper-mill. If he hadn't been so big, I'd licked him. I an't very stout, neither, though

I'm full in the face. As the boys say, "I'm fat as a match and healthy as the small-pox." It's getting cold down here; wonder how I'll get out? I an't able to climb; if I had a drink, I think I could do it. Let's see, I an't got three cents. Wish I was in a tavern; I could sponge it then. When anybody treats, and says, "Come, fellers!" I always thinks my name is fellers, and I've too good manners to refuse. I must leave this place, or I'll be arrested for burglary, and I an't come to that yet. Anyway, it was the wheelbarrow did the harm, and not me!

A. BURNETT.

A CHILD'S VOW.

CIDER I will not sip,
It shall not pass my lip,
Because it has made drunkards by the score.
The apples I will eat,
But cider, hard or sweet,
I will not touch, or taste, or handle more.

The ruddy-red wine-cup
I never will lift up,
A snake is coiled beneath the gleaming wine—
A deadly, poison thing,
And he will bite and sting;
I see his fierce eyes through the bubbles shine.

I will not taste of gin,
It leads to vice and sin;
And so do brandy, ale, and rum, and beer.
But God has made a drink
Better than all, I think—
Cold water; that we never need to fear.

It does not steal our brains,
It does not give us pains,
It quenches thirst, and does not leave a sting.
That is the drink for me—
Cold water, pure and free,
That gushes from the pearly mountain-spring.

ELLA WHEELER.

BE BRAVE, MY BROTHER!

BE brave, my brother!
And let the wine-cup pass;
Gird up thy strength, for much it needs
To shun the social glass.
It may be a beauty's hand
That proffereth it to thee;
Put on thine armor to withstand
Such twofold witchery.
'Tis not alone the battle-field
That needs a hero true,
There's many a strife in calmer life
That needs a hero too.
Then be brave, my brother,
And let the wine-cup pass;
Gird up thy strength, for much it needs
To shun the social glass.

Be strong, my brother,
Refuse the glowing cup,
Although it needs thy utmost strength
Sometimes to give it up.
Where genial spirits meet,
And friends around thee press,
Put on thine armor to defend
Thy path in gentleness.

For many a joyous feast
  And hospitable board
May prove as rife with battle strife
  As battle-fields afford.
    But be strong, my brother,
      Refuse the glowing cup,
    Although it takes thy utmost strength
      Sometimes to give it up.

Be firm, my brother,
  And joys will soon be thine;
The joys of peace and happiness
  Surpass the joys of wine.
To help destroy the serpent's sting,
  Make bare the lion's den,
Removing much that's dangerous
  From 'mongst thy fellow-men;
'Tis surely worth the striving for,
  And worth thy ablest powers,
To clear the way for better days
  In this fair world of ours.
    Then be firm, my brother,
      And joys will soon be thine—
    The joys of peace and happiness,
      Surpassing joys of wine.

Objections Against Abstinence.

Hardly any sensible person now defends drinking upon the old plan; but when any one speaks about total abstinence or temperance, the usual mode is to "trot out" some objection against it, and then to endeavor to ride off upon that objection. It is common, for example, to say, "Why, wine is a creature of God, and what could it have been for but drinking? and if it be a creature of God, therefore it is plain that men must be held to be warranted in using it." It is sufficient to say that there are many creatures of God to the use of which it is proper to set a limit. Arsenic, for example, is very useful in the arts and sciences, very useful in medicine, and is used by young girls, it is alleged, in Styria in beautifying the skin; but every one knows perfectly well that there are certain limits set, not merely by the common sense of the individual, but by the law, to the use of arsenic. It regulates its sale, and, in many countries, the form and the quantity in which it shall be sold are prescribed. And if it be right and proper to set these limits, and on the part of men to submit to them, it is conceivable that it may be equally right and just and proper to fix a certain limit to the use of this particular creature, and to confine all men and women that have respect to their comfort and welfare within those certain and definite limits. Well, but it is undeniably said that the Bible records the case of many people who use wine, and there is no explicit condemnation of their use of it. Suppose we concede that for a moment; there is no difficulty about it. You must be ready to admit, on the other hand, that in many places the Bible explicitly condemns the abuse of wine; it explicitly speaks against strong drink; it denounces it in the strongest language of which we know. Well, but it is said on the part of some: "You take the case of a good man like Timothy. Now, it is unquestionable that Timothy is expressly enjoined by the inspired writer to use a little wine for his stomach's sake and for his often infirmities." I think that is the one text which the opponents of total abstinence know the best in the whole Bible. Indeed, it seems to me that if they had the making of a kind of eclectic Bible, that and two or three other texts would be about the whole of it. But it appears to me that they entirely misapprehend the force and meaning of that statement. If one judges that statement correctly, it comes substantially to this: That whether he was right or wrong about the matter, Timothy's ordinary habit had been to drink water, and water only. That seems to be the clear, intelligible, and fair inference from the statement. But now an exceptional condition of his health had arisen, and, in view of that peculiar state of his health, the Apostle Paul, reflecting that wisdom and consideration by which the Bible is everywhere characterized, says, "Use no longer water, but use a little wine for thy stomach's sake and for thine often infirmities." And we should do precisely the same thing. We should not feel as an ordinary matter that there was anything in our principles of Christian temperance that interfered with our endorsing or accepting the counsel that was thus given; but I would emphatically make it a *very little* wine for one's stomach sake. If any one is inclined to insist upon pushing the Scripture argument, there is another view that I would commend to the consideration of thoughtful people. Men will say to us, "Ah! yes, everybody is agreed that the *abuses* of the thing are very bad." There was a day within the memory of some here when people did not talk about the abuses, but they have been carried over that. They all admit the abuses are very bad; they say, "Why don't you total abstinence people keep hammering at the *abuses?* Why do you talk so much against the *uses?*" Well, now, upon that subject there is something for fair and candid people to take into account. Is it not conceivable that the frequent use of a thing may become attended with evils so near, so palpable, so many, and so serious, that it will be wise for a good man to consider whether he ought not to forego even the use? Was not that practically the condition in which the Apostle Paul found himself in another matter? Was not that practically the state of things that he contemplated when he said, "If meat make my brother to offend, I shall eat no meat while the world standeth?" Was not that practically his state of mind in another case when he said, "It is good neither to eat flesh, nor to drink wine, nor anything whereby thy brother stumbleth, or is offended, or is made weak?" Does any man in his senses question that there are hundreds and thousands and tens of thousands of people made weak, made to stumble, and destroyed by the use of this thing?

REV. JOHN HALL, D.D.

THE DRINK! THE DRINK!

COME near, all ye who have learned to think,
And hear me speak of the drink, the drink;
Come, male and female; come, age and youth,
And list while I tell the simple truth.
It's bad for the brain, it's bad for the nerves,
For the man that buys and the man that serves;
It's bad for the eyes, and it's bad for the breath,
It's bad for life, and it's worse for death;
It's bad for the pocket, it's bad for the fame,
It's bad when often it bears no blame;
It's bad for friendship, it's worse for strife,
It's bad for the husband, it's bad for the wife;
It's bad for the face, where the pimples come,
It's bad for the children, and bad for the home;
It's bad when the tradesman's bill's to pay,
It's bad—oh! how bad—for a "rainy day";
It's bad when it nerves a man to do
The crime that he's not accustomed to.
It was bad for the culprit who sighs in jail,
It's bad for his wife—so pale, so pale;
It's bad for the strong, and it's bad for the weak,
For the sallow tinge that it lends to the cheek;

It's bad when the social glass we take,
And bad next morning when we awake;
It's bad for the day when you pay rent,
And bad for the child with the pitcher sent;
It is bad for the young who schooling lack,
And bad for the clothes on the drunkard's back;
The ruffian's joy, the murderer's hope,
The passport oft to the hangman's rope;
It's bad, as myriads who moan below,
Could they once return, would be fain to show;
It's bad in the morning, it's bad at night,
Though the talk is loud, and the fire burns bright;
It's bad, for it leads from bad to worse—
Not only bad, but a giant curse;
The poor man's bane, destruction's gate,
The church's shame, the blight of the state;
A poison fly, with a venomous sting,
That makes our glory a tainted thing.

Pitcher or Jug?

WHICH, in the heat of noontide sun,
Which, when the work of day is done,
Refreshes most the weary one,
Pitcher or jug?

Which makes strong to cradle the grain,
Which heaps highest the harvest train,
Which gives muscle and heart and brain,
Pitcher or jug?

Which sows kindness over the soil,
Lighting the heavy hours of toil,
With friendly words that never roil,
Pitcher or jug?

The pitcher, filled from the bubbling spring,
Playing and spraying,
Curling and whirling,
Over the pebbles, under the hill.
It cools the brow and steadies the brain,
Making the faint one strong again.
For its daily task it nerves the arm,
And lends to labor a borrowed charm.
It is a step on the road to wealth—
Many a step in the way of health.
It lightens home with a cheerful glow,
And banishes from it useless woe;
It smiles on the children's winsome ways,
And leaves no sting on the holidays;
So in all the best things a man will be richer
If he gives up the jug, and drinks from the pitcher.

NO MAN HAS A RIGHT TO BE NEUTRAL.

NO man has a right to be neutral in the great work of temperance, at this age, and in this country. Every man, from considerations of personal safety, from moral considerations, from considerations of his relations to his fellow-men in social life, and from considerations of patriotism or of state, ought to take sides in this matter, and let his position be known of all men. It is too notorious to require any proof that, to a very great extent, especially in the cities, our legislation begins in the grog-shop. The seed of judges is planted there. Our administrations spring out of the ooze and mud of drinking-holes. Our national councils are begun there. The machinery of government is arranged there. There is no part of the community so active as that which lives in the indulgence of the animal appetites; and there is no part of the community which should be watched over with such sleepless vigilance by those who, by sound morality and superior judgment, are fitted to wisely administer the affairs of the nation. And the time has come when all good men, who have so long staid at home, and left the management of political affairs in the hands of dissipated and unscrupulous men, should come together, and take the side of purity and temperance. We must produce a radical change in the public sentiment of the country on this vital question, or we shall be destroyed by the overwhelming deluge of the drinking habits of society.

H. W. BEECHER.

VOTE IT OUT.

THERE'S a nuisance in the land,
Rank with age and foul with crime,
Strong with many a legal band,
Sanctioned by the touch of time;
'Tis the question of the hour,
How shall we all the wrong o'erpower?
Vote it out;
This will put the thing to rout.

We have begged the traffic long,
Begged it both with smiles and tears,
To abate the flood of wrong,
But it answered us with sneers;
We are weary of the scourge,
This the way at last we urge:
Vote it out;
Loyal people, raise the shout.

'Tis the battle of the hour.
Freemen, show your strength again;
In the ballot is your power,
This will bring the foe to pain;
We have preached against the wrong,
Argued, plead, with words of song;
Votes are stout,
Let us vote the traffic out.

Vote it out of decency;
Vote it down a craven crime;
Let the fearful traffic be
Branded for all coming time;
Draw the lines of right, and stand,
Christian man, and show your hand;
Vote it out,
Join it with your prayer devout.

While the broken-hearted pray,
Where the bitterest tears are poured,
In low anguish every day,
In the sight of God, the Lord,
Let us pray and say "Amen,"
Lifting holy hands, and then
Vote it out;
It will bring the victor's shout.

Never shall the promise fail,
God is with us for the right;
Truth is mighty to prevail,
Faith shall end in joyous sight;
We shall see the hosts of rum
Palsied with affright and dumb;
Vote it out,
This will put the trade to rout.

Streams of Pure Water.

When Adam, the first of our ill-doing race,
Was sent into Eden, that beautiful place,
He drank of pure water, and thought no disgrace
    To drink of the streams of pure water.

The whiskey may stir up your fancy awhile,
But there's stuff in a glass all your visions to spoil;
And he that would still have his face wear a smile
    Must drink of the streams of pure water.

Had Noah drunk water when wine was his fare,
He had not been laughed at, as people declare;
But wine he would have, and more than his share—
    He cared not for springs of pure water.

So, good people, now it is plain to be seen,
As the boys say that live in Old Erin the green,
"That lumps of misfortune are kegs of poteen,"
    But joy is in streams of pure water.

Then here's to pure water, the life of the land,
On honor's bright bosom it ne'er laid a brand;
And we, while it circles our dear rocky strand,
    Will sing of the streams of pure water.

Moral Sentiment.

After the victories of half a century, we at last confront a moral foe whose dominion is co-extensive with the abode and business of man. What pre-eminent question is now before the moral world? Is it personal liberty? Domestic slavery has been destroyed from continent and island. The black man has risen to the dignity and to the immunities of manhood. In our own country he stands side by side with the Caucasian; and whatever rights yet remain for him to enjoy he will soon receive.

What remains now for us to do? What great cause is to engage the affections, the zeal, the attention of all good persons in the church and out of the church? I hold that that pre-eminent cause is the cause of temperance—a cause that carries its interests to the abode of every man; for the evils of intemperance are co-extensive with the home of every human being. Those evils are not confined to our Republic. They are felt through South America and Central America; they are realized in all the great capitals of Europe; they are experienced in Asia, Africa, and in the islands of the sea. Much has been accomplished, but much remains to be done. Some great facts are worthy of our cognizance, because they have received the approbation of every candid mind; and first of all, the power and the wisdom of personal effort and of moral suasion in this great moral enterprise. I question whether there are two persons in any Christian land who disagree touching the power and the practicability of persuading men by personal effort to abandon the intoxicating cup.

The law of limitation is as prevalent as law itself. This universe, from atoms to worlds, is subject to law, and atoms and worlds are subject to the limitations of law. Absolute liberty does not exist in God's universe ; it cannot co-exist with God as the sovereign of the universe. Therefore, there must be a limit to law. What now remains to be accomplished? The creation of an intelligent and permanent moral sentiment touching this great cause; for back of constitutions, and back of laws, and back of administrations, there lies a moral sentiment which gives potency to law and authority to government. This fair Republic of ours would go to pieces, like a rope of sand, were it not for the existence and the sustaining of a moral sentiment in this country. I hold that this country is not governed so much by law as it is by moral sentiment. Moral sentiment here is more potent than government itself. It is moral sentiment that turns out the thieves and robbers from your city governments. Moral sentiment may be in a minority, but whenever moral sentiment is aroused on the side of right, it assumes the proportion of omnipotence, and it is equal to any and every emergency. Wickedness is always cowardly. One of the greatest of men has said, "The wicked flee when no man pursueth," and one gifted with a genius as great, has said on the opposite side,

> "Thrice armed is he who hath his quarrel just;
> And he but naked, though locked up in steel,
> Whose conscience with injustice is corrupted."

We wish, therefore, to create an intelligent and permanent moral sentiment on two things: first, that intemperance is an evil, only evil, and always evil, whether in the form of moderate drinking or in the form of habitual drunkenness. We want to create an intelligent permanent moral sentiment that civil law should be on the side of this grand cause. Where and how shall this moral sentiment be created?

REV. J. P. NEWMAN.

Where are You Going, Young Man?

WHERE are you going so fast, young man?
Where are you going so fast?
With a cup in your hand, a flush on your brow,
Though pleasure and mirth may accompany you now,
It tells of a sorrow to come by-and-by,
It tells of a pang that is sealed with a sigh,
It tells of a shame at last, young man—
A withering shame that will last.

Where are you going so fast, young man?
Where are you going so fast?
The flush of that wine there is only a bait,
A curse lies beneath that you'll find when too late;
A serpent sleeps down in the depths of that cup,
A monster is there that will swallow you up;
A sorrow you'll find at last, young man—
In wine there is sorrow at last.

Sorrow you'll find in that cup, young man,
A giant lurks in that bright sparkle and foam,
To rob you of manhood, of friends, and of home,
To make you a brute, and to rob you of peace,
To bind you in chains with no chance of release;
You die if you drink it up, young man—
You die if you drink it up.

There's a reckoning day to come, young man,
A reckoning day to come,
A life yet to live, and a death yet to die,
A sad parting tear and a parting sigh,
A journey to take, and a famishing heart,
A sharp pang to feel from death's chilling dart,
A curse if you drink that rum, young man—
Bitterest curse in that rum,

Then halt in your mad career, young man,
Halt in your maddened career,
And read the sad warning beneath the wine,
For this is the sentence, line upon line:
Disaster and misery, sorrow and fear,
Ruin, disgrace, and the world's taunting jeer,
A soul that is lost with a leer, young man,
A soul that is lost with a leer.

THE YEAR THAT IS TO COME.

WHAT are we going to do, dear friends,
In the year that is to come,
To baffle that fearful fiend of death
Whose messenger is rum?
Shall we fold our hands and bid him pass,
As he has passed heretofore,
Leaving his deadly-poisoned draught
At every unbarred door?

What are we going to do, dear friends?
Still wait for crime and pain,
Then bind the bruises, and heal the wound,
And soothe the woe again?
Let the fiend still torture the weary wife,
Still poison the coming child,
Still break the suffering mother's heart,
Still drive the sister wild?

Still bring to the grave the gray-haired sire,
Still martyr the brave young soul,
Till the waters of death, like a burning stream,
O'er the whole great nation roll,

And poverty take the place of wealth,
  And sin, and crime, and shame
Drag down to the very depths of hell
  The highest and proudest name?

Is this our *mission* on earth, dear friends,
  In the years that are to come?
If not, let us rouse and do our work
  Against this spirit of rum.
There is not a soul so poor and weak,
  In all this goodly land,
But against this evil a word may speak,
  And lift a warning hand.

And lift a warning hand, dear friends,
  With a cry for her home and hearth,
Adding voice to voice, till the sound shall sweep,
  Like rum's death-knell, o'er the earth,
And the weak and wavering shall hear,
  And the faint grow brave and strong,
And the true, and good, and great, and wise
  Join hands to right this wrong.

Till a barrier of bold and loving hearts
  So deep and broad, is found,
That no spirit of rum can overleap,
  Pass through, or go around.
Then the spirit of rum shall surely die;
  For his food is human lives,
And only on hourly sacrifice
  The demon lives and thrives.

And can we not do this, dear friends,
  In the years that are to come?
Let each one work to save and keep
  Her loved ones and her home;

Then the ransomed soul shall send to heaven
  A song without alloy,
And "the morning stars together sing,
  And God's sons shout for joy."

MRS. F. D. GAGE.

DRINKING FOR HEALTH.

OUR homes are becoming fountain-heads of drunkenness. Wines and other drinks are on the tables, not only on special occasions, but regularly; and wives, mothers, and sisters, instead of frowning upon their use, encourage it by their example. How common it is for gentlemen in the chop-houses and restaurants to call for liquor at lunch, while at home they daily use wine or ale—"as a *medicine*," of course!

Now, what is the cause of this drift towards drinking for health? And who is directly responsible for it? *The people themselves* are chiefly responsible. They acquiesce in alcoholic prescriptions by the medical profession, and support by their patronage the villanous compounds which would otherwise prove profitless. Mothers are knowingly giving liquors in some shape to their infants (besides taking it themselves), and tens of thousands of otherwise sensible people have come to believe that they must have some strong drink.

A little must be taken for "weakness of the stomach," and a "faintness" and "goneness" of feeling when they get up. It must be sipped with the lunch, and drunk after dinner to "help digestion"; and they must have a "night-cap" before they go to bed! It would be a curious spectacle if the cellars, vaults, closets, and garrets of all the houses around us were to disgorge the filled and empty bottles that they contain, marked with some inscriptions of porter, ale, wine, tonics, bitters, and the like!

But you say, "I take a little stimulant *to help digestion.*" Then you are behind the day—you are not posted; for the popular fallacy you hold is now thoroughly exploded. Do you not *preserve* things—that is, keep them from dissolution—by alcohol, as when you preserve a piece of meat or an animal or a reptile in it? The truth is that stimulants *hinder* digestion. The stomachs of men dying after two days' steady drunkenness have been opened, and the food was found wholly undigested—*preserved*, as snakes are, in alcohol! Mix gastric juice into crushed meat, and it readily dissolves; put in beer or wine instead, and it dissolves but little; put in alcohol, and you *preserve* it! This tells the story.

If you say a glass of brandy or light wine gives *relief* after an excessive meal, I will tell you why: *not* because digestion is aided, but because the stomach is *narcotized* or *stupefied.* The nerves are deadened for the time, and, therefore, you do not feel pain. The same is true when a sense of hunger and exhaustion from want of food is relieved by a drink of spirits. In both cases, a few drops of laudanum or a small dose of morphine would produce a precisely similar effect.

Settle it in the mind, then, that no spirituous liquors can be conducive to good health. They do not give strength; they do not add warmth to the blood; they do not assist digestion. The best trainers strictly forbid their use to those striving for the highest physical development; and the brute creation are healthy without them. "In the *natural* world, the blackbird, thrush, canary, and nightingale drink nothing but water, and smoke nothing but fresh air. A grove or wood in spring echoes with feathered musicians, each a teetotaler, ever singing, and never dry."

Preposterous is it to imagine that men will thrive on what no other living thing can be made to touch!

REV. H. C. FISH.

One Night with Gin.

I'll take some sugar and gin, if you please;
I've a hacking cough perhaps 'twill ease;
Exposed myself yesterday; caught a severe cold—
And something warm—for it's good, I am told.

Some say it's injurious; and no doubt it is
To men who can't drink and attend to their biz;
I have my opinion of men who cannot
Drink now and then without being a sot.

Wasting their lives, stunting their brains,
Binding their families in poverty's chains,
Seeking a bed in the gutter, like swine,
Forgetting they're human for whiskey and wine.

But of course you don't sell to that class of men;
Don't blame you—correct—there's nothing in them;
They're a damage to trade; they injure your bar
More than their purses contribute, by far.

Another glass, if you please; that's excellent gin;
My cough I think 's better than when I came in;
Import this yourself? From Holland, you say?
Like your taste for pure drinks. Here's a V; take
your pay.

By the Temperance Society I'm annoyed and perplexed,
Coaxed to join their society until I am vexed—
A piece of absurdity too foreign to think,
That one can't indulge in a good social drink.

Over myself I know I've control,
I can sip now and then from the rich, flowing bowl,
Drink or not drink, do either with ease—
What a pity all men can't do as they please!

Have a drink, did you say? Thank you, here's luck;
That's the genuine article—no common truck.
When I start, prepare me a flask of that old,
For I'm certain it's helping my terrible cold.

So fill up the glasses, and now drink with me,
I've plenty of money—if you don't believe it, see;
Look at these fifties, these twenties, this ten;
Here's to you, drink hearty, and (hic) fill 'em again.

Stranger, (hic) I'm getting tired on my feet,
So let's fill up and drink, (hic) then find a seat.
(Hic) I like your appearance, (hic) can see in your face
That confidence in you is never misplaced.

With your permission, I'll (hic) rest here a spell,
For, mister, (hic) the fact is, I'm not (hic) feeling well.
Guess you may give me (hic) a glass of that best;
I think it's first-rate for a cold (hic) in the chest.

Heavy eyes, heavy heart, thirsty, and mad;
The gin is all gone, the head's feeling bad;
The tongue's dry and parched; he calls for a drink
To waken his wits and help him to think.

Then looks for his friend, the one of last night,
So winning and pleasant, so kind and polite;
But he's gone, and a rough-looking man's in his
place,
With a dark, evil eye and a coarse, bearded face.

He's told that his "*friend,*" so genial and witty,
Receiving a despatch, has just left the city;
The wretched young man then feels for his purse,
Only to ejaculate "*Gone!*" with a curse.

He appeals to the bar, charges robbery, theft,
Calls for the man he's informed has just left,
Then gently reminded they do not permit
Their establishment cursed in a mad drunken fit;

That he never lost money, had none to lose,
Himself a thief, vagabond, thus to abuse
A respectable house, where gentlemen come
To socially quaff their ale, gin, and rum.

Then rudely cast in the cold, open street,
Moneyless, hungry, nothing to eat—
No food for thought but reflection of shame,
And a head half-crazed with a sobering pain.

PROHIBITION.

I'M a thorough-going temperance man;
The crimes and woes of the world I scan;
I pity its hard condition;
The fountain of wrong I'd for ever dry,
To stop the flow, I'd stop the supply—
And this is prohibition.

If I knew a baker so badly bold
That in every loaf of bread he sold
Was arsenic, in secret glutition,
I'd oven him up in stone walls four,
Where he could peddle out death no more—
And this is prohibition.

If a butcher I saw in the market street
Who murdered the people with putrid meat,
The infamous scn of perdition!
I'd stall him where his stand would be sure,
His bread all plain, and his water pure—
And this is prohibition.

If I heard a serpent hid in the grass,
Who stung every traveller certain to pass,
I'd curb his thirsty ambition;
An iron heel on his head I'd bring,
I'd crush out his life with its devilish sting—
And this is prohibition.

If I had a fold, where the wolf crept in,
And ate up my sheep and lambs, like sin,
I'd hold him in tight partition;
I'd choke the howl of his tainted breath,
And save my flock by his instant death—
And this is prohibition.

If an ox, let loose in a crowded lawn,
Were wont to kill with his angry horn,
All heedless of mortal petition;
I'd cleave his skull with a swift-swung ax,
And bury his horn in his bloody tracks—
And this is prohibition.

If I met a dog that was wont to bite,
Who worried my neighbors, day and night,
I'd fix him by demolition!
In spite of his waggings, and yelpings, and tears,
I'd cut off his tail just back of his ears—
And this is prohibition.

REV. C. W. DENISON.

BEWARE!

ALL inspiration combines to give fearful and impressive warning. From this very inspired Word, where God declares that no drunkard should enter the kingdom of heaven, there comes a voice from the Infinite lips saying to you and to me and to all: "Beware, beware!" In that land where the streets are gold, and the gates are pearl, and the walls are jasper and sapphire, the finger of God has written, "No drunkard shall enter here." No drunkard shall sit down in the kingdom of heaven. I know not why it is there. It may be because he has voluntarily debased the image of God in which he was created. It may be because he has given himself up to the temptation which leads one away from that which is of good report, virtuous, and just. But whatever may be the reason, from that book which never errs comes this warning to us, "Beware!" To you it says, "Beware!" To the moderate drinker it says, "Beware!" The man you met this afternoon reeling in his cups on the sidewalk—the man you have seen drinking at the counter of the lowest saloon, began just as you begin. Poor-houses and prisons say to you, "Beware!" They whose arms were nerve, and whose forms were grace, to-day, dead from intoxication, say to you, with their gloomy lesson, "Beware!" Homes once happy, now miserable; wives once joyous in the love of their husbands, now turned to hatred, while the caresses of the husband are turned to abuse, and competence to poverty, from the midst of their miseries and desolation warn you and exclaim, "Beware!"

Choose you this day whether you and yours will stand with us on the rock of safety, above the snares, and evil, and anguish, and misery, and woe, and desolation of the tempter; whether, defying the warnings that nature and inspiration combine to give, you will go down, down, after the first step (for it is always the first that costs), that easy descent, until at last, wretched and dishonored, having lost the respect of others and your own self-respect, you end a miserable life by a home in a tomb, from which there is, if inspiration be true, no resurrection that shall take you to a better land. Does not your hope for happiness here and hereafter give emphasis to that one word which embodies all I can say to you, which comes from God's own lips, "Beware"?

SCHUYLER COLFAX.

FILLED WITH WINE.

THE following ode was written by L. M. Sargent, the distinguished author of "Sargent's Temperance Tales," in 1837, for the Massachusetts Temperance Society, based on the following passage of Scripture:

"Thou shalt speak unto them this word: Thus saith the Lord God of Israel, Every bottle shall be filled with wine; and they shall say unto thee, Do we not certainly know that every bottle shall be filled with wine? Then shalt thou say unto them, Thus saith the Lord, Behold, I will fill all the inhabitants of this land, even the kings that sit upon David's throne, and the priests, and the prophets, and all the inhabitants of Jerusalem, with drunkenness. And I will dash them one against another, even the fathers and the sons together, saith the Lord; I will not pity, nor spare, nor have mercy, but destroy them."—Jeremiah xiii; 12—14.

When Israel's God in his anger had spoken,
The prophet prefigured the curse that he willed;
It was not that life's golden bowl should be broken,
But every bottle with wine should be filled.

The priest of the altar, besotted and sunken,
Was wrapped in the vengeance that Heaven had hurled;
Kings, prophets, and patriarchs drank, and were drunken—
The grape's purest juice was the curse of the world.

Their bottles were filled with the nectar that gladdens
  The heart, which the patriarch drew from the vine;
And not with that tincture of ruin that maddens—
  God's vials of wrath were their bottles of wine!

Avert, God of mercy, that sorrow and sadness
  That broke the fond hearts of Jerusalem then;
Permit not the spirit of murder and madness
  To move with the form and the features of men!

Oh! let us not torture the treasures of heaven
  To find where the secret of misery lies;
The stream as it ripples, the rock that is riven,
  The pure draught of nature for mortal supplies.

The bonds of the bacchanal hence let us sever,
  The draught that bewilders the reason, resign;
The type of the prophet be cherished for ever—
  God's vials of wrath were their bottles of wine!

Never Begin.

In going down-hill on a slippery track,
The going is easy, the task getting back;
But you'll not have a tumble, a slip, nor a stop,
Nor toil from below, if you stay at the top.

  So from drinking, and swearing, and every sin,
  You are safe and secure if you never begin;
  Then never begin! never begin!
  You cannot be a drunkard unless you begin.

So in mounting a ladder, or scaling a wall,
You may climb to the top, or be bruised by a fall;
My philosophy's this, and I think it is sound:
If not needed above, to remain on the ground.

Some boast they can stand on the cataract's brink—
Some do it, but some topple over and sink;
Then I think, to be safe, the most sensible plan
Is to keep from the brink just as far as you can.

In a journey you may have to make the descent,
By climbing, a danger to others prevent;
You may rescue the child from the rock's giddy shelf,
But never save sinners by sinning yourself.
So from drinking, and swearing, and every sin,
You are safe and secure if you *never* begin.

EDWARD CARSWELL.

SHALL WE FAIL?

Soldiers of the Temperance army! gird yourselves, for the conflict is not over. Behold the bar-rooms in our midst. See their fiery contents as they stand like some burning volcanos, and we know not at what moment we may be overwhelmed by them. Oh! shall we slumber beneath the fires of Vesuvius and Etna, and be not alarmed?

Methinks I hear the cry of fire, fire! rolling from the sultry belt to either pole. The world is on fire! burning up with the liquid fire—more terrific in its march than the Chicago flames! The cold-water army is on its march to extinguish the fire. If we succeed, we will proclaim a year of Jubilee—the world redeemed from the curse of dissipation.

"Shout, earth! shout, heaven!"

Then I would want our planet environed with a zodiac of unfading rainbow splendor, and inscribed on it, over either continent, in every dialect of earth, in burning characters, the golden inscription, "The world is redeemed from the curse of dissipation." That all nations might sit beneath the soul-cheering ark, and shout and sing the song of that redemption at once and for ever! Then the angels that in their flight from world to world bend their course to shun this bedlam of the universe, will turn out of their way to visit a second Paradise. Then will the temperance orders bathe our planet in an atmosphere of perfume "sweeter than Arabia sacrificed, and the spicy mountains in a flame."

On the other hand, if we are finally overrun with drunkenness, when the vision of the "black horse" shall appear, then will I ask his "rider" to release me from the horrid scenes that will ensue. The land of inebriates! the drunkard's planet! Let all nature mourn at the thought. Let the verdure of earth be withered, and the continent dressed in black, the ocean covered in sackcloth, and the heavens spread with mourning! Then let this dark planet be rolled down to the black portals of perdition, where men and devils, exchanging visits, may claim each other as appropriate neighbors.

That total abstinence may ever peal in your ear, let my last word be abstain. May the angel, conscience, ever and anon whisper in your ear—abstain; breezes of earth bear it across the continent—abstain; billows of ocean roll it to the distant shores—abstain; heavens above congeal and echo back in world-wide thunder tones—abstain!

WATSON M. VAUGHAN.

COME AND JOIN US.

OH! not with the fife and the murderous knife,
  And the rolling sound of the battle-drum,
And the dreadful waste of human life,
  Do the glowing ranks of our army come;

But merrily, right merrily,
  And cheerily we go,
So readily and steadily,
  To battle with the foe.

With glad voice of song we are moving along,
  While the breezes soft on our banners blow;
'Tis the children's army, brave and strong,
  And we march where the clear running waters flow:
O'er mountain side the fountain tide
  In bounding pride is seen,
Now leaping down and sweeping down
  Through all the meadows green.

Ho! boys, and ye girls with the soft, sunny curls,
  Come and join the band of the brave and fair;
See our banner—look! how bright it unfurls,
  Perfumed by the kiss of the fragrant air;
Unite with us, to fight with us,
  And smite with us the foe;
Then, wondering and thundering,
  He'll tumble at the blow.

There's no one so young but can battle with wrong,
  There is no one living too old to mend;
Come and help to slay the monster strong,
  And the reign of King Alcohol shall end.
We'll water him and slaughter him,
  And bury him full low,
Beyond the reach of all who teach
  The drunkard's way to go.

GEORGE S. BURLEIGH.

"PURE LIQUOR."

DIED on Friday, the paper said,
Of delirium tremens, kind-hearted Fred.
Simple the words, but they tell a tale
Which makes the faces of men grow pale;
That chills the blood and freezes the heart,
As they dream and wake with a feverish start
At thought of the maniac, fettered and bound,
Of the heart-broken family weeping around,
Mourning for him once so cheery and strong;
Weeping for him who was father so long;
Working steady and working well,
With ceaseless clang the hammer fell;
We heard it clear on the morning air,
At eve it told us Fred was there;
For twenty years scarce missing a day,
Early and late, the neighbors say.
Once a faithful husband, a father kind,
Then a raging maniac, body and mind;
A liquid hell in his burning veins,
Racked and torn by distorting pains,
Cowering and shrinking in trembling dread
From the conjured monster with hydra-head;
Raving and cursing when the fever burns,
Moans and prays when reason returns;
His throbbing temples seeming to burst—
Slowly dying with the terrible thirst;
Slowly, surely; passing away;
Slowly changing from flesh to clay.
Again delirium howls and reels
At sight of terrors it sees and feels;
He struggles to close, in deadly strife,
With the famishing demon that seeks his life.
He falls and falls; with a last, long cry,
Evil has won, and he must die.

The gasping breath—the end comes soon—
Silence falls in that death-laden room;
A hollow rattle, a quiver—he's dead!
All that was earthly of our neighbor Fred.
And they've taken him over on the Island Hill;
There he is lying now, cold and still.

A Word of Warning.

DOUBTLESS you are ready to say that you stand in no danger from intemperance! So have numbers before you thought, whose last days were days of anguish and wretchedness, the ark of whose ruined fortunes has floated upon a sea of tears, shed by a broken-hearted and sorrowing wife, or by an aged father and mother, whose gray hairs had been brought to the grave in mourning and grief. Can there be any moderate and safe use of ardent spirits? You might as well talk of carrying a torch into a magazine of powder, where a single spark would rend the earth. Suppose as many lives were lost by the cars on our railroads as are lost by intemperance yearly, in the state; who would step aboard a single one of them? Why, you would call him a madman who would dare place his foot upon one of them; yet you think nothing of entering the Car of Intemperance, whose boilers are every day bursting, scattering death and misery in all directions. Remember that small beginnings lead to great results. Stephen Girard was once a penniless vagabond; the small stream in the snowy climes of the north becomes the mighty Mississippi when it reaches the sunny borders of the south. The drop of ardent spirits taken in youth swells to the giant in mature age; the temperate drinker in the morn of life becomes the ruined inebriate in the end.

The Children's Army.

A WORD to the little children,
  The children good and true;
Come, join the temperance army,
  And fight the battle through.
Here's wine, and beer, and cider—
  Fair little snakes that creep
Around our own dear hearth-stones,
  And fatten while we sleep.

Boys, *set your heel upon them,*
  Don't toy with them, I pray;
For they'll *sting* you while you pet them,
  While they seem in sportive play.
Here's the dirty page, *Tobacco,*
  Who waits on the *rum-king,*
And to his treacherous clutches
  Does many a victim bring.

Don't take a filthy meerschaum
  Or odorous cigar
Into your rosy lips, boys;
  'Twere better, sirs, by far
To lose your tops and marbles,
  Your skates and treasures fine,
Than to lose your *hope of manhood*
  In tobacco or in wine.

A true and noble boyhood
  Will make a manhood fine;
Then shun the treacherous cider,
  Tobacco, ale, and wine,

And join you all together
  In a legion good and true,
To fight for truth and temperance
  Till you see the battle through.

MRS. E. J. RICHMOND.

THE LITTLE BOY'S SONG.

LADIES and gentlemen,
  List to my song—
Huzza! for temperance
  All the day long!
I'll taste not, handle not,
  Touch not the wine;
For every little boy, like me,
  The temperance pledge should sign.

I am a temperance boy
  Just four years old,
And I love temperance
  Better than gold.
I'll taste not, handle not,
  Touch not the wine;
For every little boy, like me,
  The temperance pledge should sign.

Let every little boy
  Remember my song,
For God loves little boys
  That never do wrong.
I'll taste not, handle not,
  Touch not the wine;
For every little boy, like me,
  The temperance pledge should sign.

THE COLD-WATER ARMY.

A SPEECH BY A YOUNG RECRUIT.

I AM a high private in the cold-water army! I joined this noble band two months ago with the brave boys you see here to-night. I enlisted for life, or until the old enemy, King Alcohol, and his army of drunkards and dram-shops are driven from our country, and peace and good-will is established all over our happy country.

But you are ready to ask me, What does such a boy as you know about drunkards or dram-shops, or old King Alcohol's army? It is true I never was drunk, and I never intend to be; but I have lived long enough to know the difference between a drunkard and a sober man, and to know what makes drunkards and what makes sober men; and so may every boy and girl who will look around them and study the teachings of nature.

Suppose we walk out upon our extensive plains and prairies, and see the stately ox, the noble horse, the playful and sporting lambs, and all the healthy and happy herds, rejoicing in their strength. I see they feed upon grass, and grow fat; but ask them what they drink, and with one united and cheerful voice they all answer: *Water!* Pure cold water—nothing else!

Again, let us ramble off through the forest, and gaze upon the majestic oaks, the stately pines, with their evergreen plumes waving in the fresh breezes of heaven, with the ten thousand varieties of fruits, foliage, and flowers, all rejoicing in their strength, beauty, and fragrance; all mingling in peace and harmony, to give a charm to nature's garden! Let us ask them what they drink; and again, with a wave of their plumes and smiling flowers, they all answer: *Water!* Pure cold water—nothing else.

And here, too, in this forest of trees, foliage, and flowers, the whole scene is animated and sweetened by the songs of the happy birds; each sporting and warbling forth its merry song, giving life and beauty to the whole scene. When I ask them what they drink, they all chatter forth in gladness: Water! Water! Pure cold water—nothing else.

But above all, when I look upon the best of men, those who are wise, pious, and prosperous, who live in loving fellowship with their families and neighbors, and on whom the church and country depend for all that is true and valuable, I watch them to see what they drink, and I find it is water, pure cold water—nothing else.

Yes, all these drink *water*, that pure beverage that God has made, and which he has so abundantly supplied to all the animate world! He showers it down from heaven! He fills our rivulets and rivers with it. It is as free as the air all breathe! It is pure and healthful to all. It is just suited to our wants and nature. There is no serpent's sting about it—no lurking adder there. This is the drink for me, boys; it will never muddle my brains nor destroy my manhood. Yes, I am a cold-water boy!

But all do not drink cold water! Let us look about and see who they are, and what they drink!

As I pass along the streets, I see men staggering, swearing, and acting very ugly in all sorts of ways, and finally falling in the muddy gutters! I slip up to them, and ask them what they drink, and they growl out, Whiskey! bad whiskey!

I see and hear of men getting drunk, fighting, shooting, and killing each other for the merest trifles, and wonder how men can act so badly; and when I enquire what they drink, I find it is whiskey and *lager!*

When you visit the prisons, penitentiaries, and all places where criminals are kept and punished, you will find they drink bad whiskey, which biteth like a serpent and stingeth like an adder.

Whiskey robs men of their brains, consumes their property, ruins their character, takes their lives, and sends their souls to ruin.

Then why will men drink such deadly stuff? There is not a buzzard in the woods, nor an old sow in the streets, that could be made to drink it, and how can any one ask me to touch it?

Come boys, all of you, and join our cold-water army, and fight manfully for the cause. We shall soon grow up to be men, sober men, and be ready for duty, let the call come from what quarter it may. Success to the cold-water cause!

My Grandpa.

Few boys have grandpas as good as mine;
  He is eighty years old, to be sure;
Yet he never meddled with whiskey or wine,
  But drank of the water pure.
He does not chew, or smoke, or snuff
Tobacco, but hates the poison stuff;
So he is hale and hearty, and hobbles about,
And, though rather lame, it is not with the gout.
Very few of his age are half so stout—
Of course he an't spry, as he used to be
When he was a boy like you and me.

He used to go out with us boys to the grove,
  To gather the nuts as they fell;
But now he's too lame, so he sits by the stove,
  And the queerest stories he'll tell
Of how, when a boy, he could climb with ease

To the very tops of the tallest trees,
And shake down the walnuts as oft as he'd please;
But now old grandpa an't smart at all,
And scarcely can climb o'er the garden wall.

He laughs at the pranks we children play,
  And seems so happy and glad;
And he tells us all about the way
  They played 'em when he was a lad;
How they built snow forts, and stormed 'em too,
How they scuffled and scrambled, and snow-balls flew,
And all the wild frolics the boys went through;
Why, boys, we laughed till our sides were sore
When he told us all this and a great deal more.

He gave us a temperance talk last week,
  About thousands destroyed by drink;
And as he talked, I saw on his cheek
  A tear, and I could but think
That perhaps some loved one, bright and fair,
A brother or son, had been caught in the snare;
Yet to ask him about it I did not dare.
But I'll tell you what, boys, I have heard enough
To make me afraid of the poison stuff.

Our lips no wine shall ever pass,
  Nor ale, to muddle our brains;
Poor swearing Sam may swallow his glass,
  And be an old bloat for his pains;
Our drink shall be of the crystal spring,
For poor-house board is not the thing,
Or the gallows' rope a desirable swing;
The poor-house, and poison, and gallows' rope
Will never be used for our "Band of Hope."

DR. CHARLES JEWETT.

Don't Drink!

Don't drink, boys, don't!
There is nothing of happiness, pleasure, or cheer
In brandy, in whiskey, in rum, ale, or beer;
If they cheer you when drank, you are certain to pay,
In headaches and crossness, the following day.
Don't drink, boys, don't!

Boys, let it alone!
Turn your back on your deadliest enemy, Drink!
An assassin disguised; nor for one moment think,
As some rashly say, that *true* women admire
The man who can boast that he's playing with fire.
Boys, let it alone!

No, boys, don't drink!
If the habit's begun, stop now! stop to-day!
Ere the spirit of thirst leads you on and away
Into vice, shame, and drunkenness. This is the goal
Where the spirit of thirst leads the slave of the bowl.
No, boys, *don't* drink!

Ella Wheeler.

Its Name is Legion.

If war has slain its thousands, intemperance has slain its tens of thousands. And where is the father who would not prefer to see his son shot down before his face, than to behold him poisoned to a degrading death by these foul harpies whom Legion has employed?

And who are the men whose fate has thus been sealed in hopeless ruin?

They are young. They were seized and bound while young. Hardly one in hundreds has passed the maturity of his earthly days. Did they begin as purposed, willing drunkards? Nothing was further from their thoughts or their desires. They have waded out most gradually, almost imperceptibly, into the deep. They then looked down upon the inebriate sot with sorrow and contempt, as others now look down upon them. They started with the drop which their fathers gave them, or with the offered glass of friendship, at noon or night, when they lacked the courage to refuse. The demon seized them when they were sheltered, as they thought, far from his abodes, and led them on, his purpose fixed, though yet unknown to them, for their final ruin.

Where did this work of ruin begin? Do not tell me at the tavern or in haunts like that. What gave to pure and innocent youth that taste for taverns? Where did they get the appetite which sought its objects and its pleasures there? You will be compelled to look back far beyond this final limit, and to feel and to acknowledge the responsibility often coming far nearer home. The moderate drinker is but an indentured apprentice to the drunkard. A gracious divine Providence may cripple his ability in his youth, and he may not thoroughly learn his trade. But the habitual glass, however apparently refined, signs his indenture. And no one who starts in the imitation of the craft. or who leads another to take a single step in its clearly-marked line, has power to define the limits of the course.

God grant that we may never live to see our sons and daughters, so precious in our sight, cast out to perish under the destroying power of this Legion demon! But if we would avoid this terrible sorrow, let us avoid all connection with the habit or the trade. Let us remember that he plucks the lambs from the flock at home, and selects the victims for his holocausts when they and theirs least expect his approach. If you will save the souls of your children from the destruction, or your selves from all participation in the ruin, banish the "accursed thing" from your habitations; lock up the tempting bottles from their sight; and neither have, nor use, nor offer upon your tables this unnecessary inducement to vice, this direct provision for impoverishment of the health, poison to the bodies, and destruction of the souls of yourselves, and your children, and your friends.

REV. STEPHEN H. TYNG, D.D.

THE YOUTHFUL ADVOCATE.

I AM but a little teetotal man,
And cannot do much, but I do what I can
    To promote the temperance cause.
I never drink ale or any such thing
As brandy or rum, wine, whiskey, or gin—
    Man's curse, and the cause of his woes.

I drink cold water, so clear and so sweet;
It quenches my thirst, gives health to my cheek,
    And brings neither sorrows nor woes.
It comes from above, so bright and so free;
In dewdrops it shines like pearls from the sea;
    And in streams of abundance it flows.

Enriching the soil, it supplies us with bread,
Gives life to the flowers in the green, grassy mead,
    And meets us where'er we may rove.
The beautiful birds, in the midst of their song,
Stop and drink from the brook as it murmurs along
    Through brake and through woodland and grove.

Would you sing, like the birds, with sweetness and
power,
Or, blooming in beauty, outrival the flower,
With cheeks fresh and healthy as mine?
Make water your drink, and unite heart and hand
To rescue and save every child in the land,
And the pledge of true temperance sign.

UNCLE POTTER.

I HAVE SIGNED THE PLEDGE.

I HAVE signed the pledge, the temperance pledge!
Such a little boy as I? you say;
Oh! yes, I am small; and so is the edge
Of your broadax; but it spreads away
To a noble head, and the chips must go
When it hews to the line with blow on blow!

I have signed the pledge, the guardian pledge,
That none who walk are too small to sign.
Too small? 'Tis the *little* end of the wedge
That starts the crack in the knotted pine;
Let it begin *there*, and it rips
The sturdiest oak into basket-strips.

I have signed the pledge, the beautiful pledge;
I will *keep* it—it keeps *me* no less;
You guard young corn with a sturdy hedge,
Our young souls need it as well, I guess:
We little blades beginning to shoot
Have a tempting look to the old black goat!

I have signed the pledge, the glorious pledge;
And though I am small and my years are few,
I grow—'tis a smart boy's privilege!—
And I'll pick up time as fast as you!
The wedge grows into me, one live bough,
As the buds you set in a sapling grow!

I have signed the pledge, the living pledge;
One chance the jail and the poor-house lose;
There's one less chance for the river-dredge
To be clogged with a sot in its dripping ooze;
And one bid more for the crown that waits
The virtuous man at the golden gates.

GEORGE S. BURLEIGH.

THE LIQUOR REVENUE.

THERE are a good many hypocrisies in the world, I am afraid; and everybody that I ever knew condemns hypocrisy. It is sometimes charged upon Christian societies; the world is uncharitable enough to do that at times.

Now, I say here, with the most perfect soberness and deliberateness, that of all the hypocrisies of which I have ever heard or read, I think the hypocrisy that affects to look with suspicion upon this movement, lest the revenue should suffer, is the most groundless, the most impudent, and the most absurd. Oh! but men say, "Look here, suppose that the whole business of drinking is put an end to, and suppose you fanatical total abstainers had your way, and we became an absolutely total abstinence people, what in the world would ever become of the United States without the revenue?" Just think of one of my countrymen (and I am sorry to say it), not particularly well clothed, blear-eyed, with face pebbled over with strawberries, turning off his glass of whiskey, or whatever other vile compound may pass under that name, and with a great look of virtue and public spirit saying, "Why, my fellow-citizens, I am doing this thing *pro bono publico*." Why, my dear friends, the thing is too absurd; and these people do not believe a word of it. But if they did and if there were any real sincerity in them, the objector can be fairly met upon his own ground. Is there any sensible man in this meeting—and there are a great many here—who does not know, upon ten minutes' reflection, that, if you could subtract to-morrow from the public funds of this country all that comes into those funds through the liquor traffic, in less than one year there would come back in various ways into those coffers, or, which is the same thing, into the substantial strength and prosperity of the country, ten times as much saved in increased honesty and fidelity, in the cost of taking care of the paupers, in the cost of detecting and punishing crime, and in the additional value that would be given to labor by the reclamation of this vast mass of our fellow-creatures who are now not a help but a burden to the community, and who, sooner or later, in one form or other, come to be a tax upon the honest and sober portion of the community? But if this be not conceded, if there is anybody so absurd as to suppose that these United States cannot stand unless they can be backed up by revenue gained from the liquor traffic, then, dearly as I love this land, dearly as I love these United States, I would say, "Let them go"; for there must be something radically and completely wrong about any great and magnificent community like this, if it cannot be maintained unless bolstered up by gains so vile and horrible as these. But some say, "There is no use of your talking in this way, the community will go on and drink as it has done in times past." That may be; but we, at least, shall be clear in our consciences. We are not, however, so despairing about that matter as might at first sight be supposed. An immensity has been done already within the memory of living people. The tide of public opinion does not roll now as it rolled fifty years ago, when it was a necessary part of an honest man's hospitality to make his neighbor drunk, if he wanted to treat him well. We shall not despair of this Christianity of ours. There is a religious system, infinitely inferior to that which we profess, which has made and kept whole populations, not merely sober, but has kept them total abstainers for generations and centuries; and I am not going to believe that what corrupt forms of thought, heathen forms, have succeeded in accomplishing it will be impossible for our Christianity, when it is living, earnest, and baptized with the Holy Ghost, to accomplish among ourselves.

REV. JOHN HALL, D.D.

"I HAVE DRUNK MY LAST GLASS."

No, comrades, I thank you, not any for me;
My last chain is riven—henceforward I'm free!
I will go to my home and my children to-night,
With no fumes of liquor their spirits to blight,
And, with tears in my I eyes I will beg my poor wife
To forgive me the wreck I have made of her life.
"I have never refused you before!" Let that pass;
For I've drunk my last glass, boys,
I have drunk my last glass!

Just look at me now, boys, in rags and disgrace,
With my bleared, haggard eyes and my red, bloated
face!
Mark my faltering step and my weak, palsied hand,
And the mark on my brow that is worse than Cain's
brand.

See my crownless old hat, and my elbows and knees,
Alike warmed by the sun or chilled by the breeze.
Why, even the children will hoot as I pass;
But I've drunk my last glass, boys,
I have drunk my last glass.

You would hardly believe, boys, to look at me now,
That a mother's soft hand was once pressed on my brow,
When she kissed me and blessed me, her darling, her pride,
Ere she lay down to rest by my dead father's side;
But, with love in her eyes, she looked up to the sky,
Bidding *me* to meet her *there*, and whispered, "Good-by."
And I'll do it, God helping! Your smile I let pass;
For I've drunk my last glass, boys,
I have drunk my last glass.

Ah! I reeled home last night—it was not very late,
For I'd spent my last sixpence, and landlords won't wait
On a fellow who's left every cent in their till,
And has pawned his last bed, their coffers to fill.
Oh! the torments I felt, and the pangs I endured!
And I begged for *one* glass—just *one* would have cured—
But they kicked me out doors! I let that, too, pass;
For I've drunk my last glass, boys,
I have drunk my last glass.

At home my pet Susie, with her golden hair,
I saw through the window, just kneeling in prayer;
From her pale, bony hands her torn sleeves were strung down,
While her feet, cold and bare, shrank beneath her scant gown;

And she prayed—prayed for *bread,* just a poor crust of bread,
For *one* crust—on her knees my pet darling plead!
And I *heard,* with no penny to buy one, alas!
But I've drunk my last glass, boys,
I have drunk my last glass.

For Susie, my darling, my wee six-year-old,
Though fainting with hunger and shivering with cold,
There, on the bare floor, asked God to bless *me!*
And she said, "Don't cry, mamma! He will; for you see
I *believe* what I ask for!" Then sobered, I crept
Away from the house; and that night when I slept,
Next my heart lay the PLEDGE! You smile, let it pass;
For I've drunk my last glass, boys,
I have drunk my last glass.

My darling child saved me! Her faith and her love
Are akin to my dear sainted mother's above!
I will make her words true, or I'll die in the race,
And sober I'll go to my last resting-place;
And she shall kneel there, and, weeping, thank God
No *drunkard* lies under the daisy-strewn sod!
Not a drop more of poison my lips shall e'er pass;
For I've drunk my last glass, boys,
I have drunk my last glass.

LOUISA S. UPHAM.

Our Cause is Christ's Cause.

I ADVOCATE temperance because it is to me the legitimate application of the Gospel to the present necessity. There are many people who say to us that we teetotalers put temperance in the place of the Gospel. I fling back the accusation with indignation and scorn. We do not put total abstinence in the place of the Gospel; but we are abstainers because we are believers in the Gospel, and because we wish to apply the truth of the Gospel to this question. Take the beautiful parable of the good Samaritan. What does it mean in regard to this matter of temperance? Come, now, my friend, let us reason together. "Go thou and do likewise." What does that mean to-day? Many people, when they come upon this command in the New Testament, imagine that it means simply that they must wait until they see a poor man in the precise circumstances in which that half-dead traveller was, and then they are to go and do for him precisely the same things as the good Samaritan did, and so they will be doing likewise. That is only a clumsy copy of the great example. That is not a real imitation of it. To get an imitation, you must go below, and lay hold of the principle; and the question which you have to face to-day is, Where shall I find in society the person who is represented by this poor, half-dead traveller, and what for me shall correspond to the oil, the wine, and the money which his benefactor gave? Where shall I find him? I find him in the little, homeless street newsboy, growing up to be a pest and a criminal in society. I open for him a lodging-house, I tend and care for him, teach him to save money, and lead him to the Lord Jesus Christ; and so I go and do likewise. I find him in the poor sickly inhabitant of your tenement-houses, and I try by all the means in my power to raise proper dwellings for the working-man; and so I go and do likewise. I find him in the poor, sinning, sorrowing sister standing by the street-corner, and I open for her a home of refuge; and so I go and do likewise. I find him in the poor helpless drunkard, groaning under his misery, and feeling terribly the weight of his chain, and I stoop down to his level, and, taking him by the hand, say, "My brother, I will abstain along with you; come, and I will try and raise thee up, by the help of God"; and so I go and do likewise. Will any one say that this is not a legitimate application of the principles of that parable, which are the principles underlying the whole Gospel of Christ?

Then, again, we find Paul saying, "If meat make my brother to offend, I will eat no flesh while the world stands. It is good neither to eat flesh nor to drink wine, nor to do anything whereby thy brother stumbleth, or is offended, or is made weak." Lay those words along the line of the present circumstances, and tell me, can they mean anything, or can they point to anything, but to such a movement as this of total abstinence? Let us, then, rejoice that we can advocate this cause beneath the cross of the Lord Jesus Christ. He who laid down his life for others says to us, "You must lay down your lives for the brethren." Yes, lives! That would be a great thing. But it is not that we are asking to-night. We are only asking that you lay down your glass. You may not find it to be a very great sacrifice after all; but, if you make it for his sake, it will be a sacrifice well pleasing in his sight. And why should not we make it for his sake, if thereby we may raise a fellow-man? You know the beautiful Old Testament story of King David, when, with one of those fits of home-sickness, as Dean Stanley calls them, which sometimes came over him, he longed vehemently for a draught of the water of Bethany, from which he drank in the shepherd days. Three of his chief captains who heard his wish dashed through the thickest of the foe, went to the spring, and brought to him a vessel of water; but he would not drink it. There were men's lives perilled for that beverage, and he poured it out before the Lord. So, when you raise your wine-cup, will you think a moment of the multitudes of human lives that are being continually sacrificed by that beverage, and will you not, David-like, pour it out before the Lord? I raise this principle to one of the highest and most sacred importance—before the Lord—Inasmuch as ye do it for one of the least of these his brethren, ye do it for himself. REV. WM. M. TAYLOR.

A TEETOTALER'S APOLOGY.

THE glass you offer I, with thanks, decline.
Thanks for your kindness. Neither ale, nor wine,
Nor fiery spirit I'll accept from thee,
As proof of cordial hospitality,
I value not the less your generous mind,
And, lest you think me churlish or unkind,
Will give the reason; and am certain you
Must then approve the act, and reason too.

I dare not taste; there's danger in the drink!
To me it seems like standing on the brink
Of that dark precipice where thousands fell,
Whose fearful histories I have studied well—
Men of repute for genius, education,
Religious teachers, rulers of the nation.
These stood as firm as we stand in our day,
And yet they lost their balance. Who can say
But we, like those whose ruin we thus see,
From the same cause may find like misery.

Do I mistrust myself? you ask. I do!
And yet I know myself as strong as you
In mind and will, my self-respect as high;
And I am sure this fact you'll not deny—
That it requires much firmness to withstand
That which is offered by your liberal hand.
It proves not mental weakness that I've signed
The temperance pledge. It needs a constant mind
To resist temptation from the friend we prize;
Not friendship's offering can a friend despise.

And here the pledge a shield is, a defence
To resist temptation. For on what pretence
Can a true friend, then, urge that thing on me
Which compromises honor?
Thus, you see,
The temperance pledge gives power to self-denial,
And strength for conflict in the day of trial;
From custom's thraldom it thus set me free:
This, then, to you is my apology.

The Natural Beverage.

THERE can be no good excuse for the habit of using intoxicating drinks. Neither fermented nor distilled liquors will quench thirst. Tipplers and topers take a sup of water after swallowing a glass of whiskey. Alcohol will not quench thirst, for it adds fuel to the fire. Water is the natural beverage of all living things, and we have a great abundance of it. It comes from the clouds in silver showers; it unwinds from the fountain like threads from a spool; it rolls in brooks and rivers at our feet; it spreads in lakes which lie like molten mirrors in vales of emerald grass and golden flowers. The flower holds its fragrant vase in green arms to catch it, and stoops from the bank to kiss the wave which flows at its feet. The bird dips its bill in a drop of rain or dew, and then lifts its little head, as though it returned thanks for the blessing. The deer and the lamb, the ox and the horse, and all living creatures whose taste has not been spoiled, drink water. It will quench thirst, and light no fever in the throat. It will do no harm to the body, to the mind, nor to the heart, nor to the soul. It is given to us pure and without color, so that we can see and taste the impurities, if any have been mixed with it. Now, my friends, let us all join the cold-water army, and sign the cold-water pledge, that our breath may be sweet as the breath of flowers, our voices as clear as the voices of the birds, and our lives as pure as the dew and the rain.

THE SEVEN AGES OF INTEMPERANCE.

ALL the world's a bar-room
And all the men and women merely tipplers;
They have their bottles and their glasses;
And one man in his turn takes many quarts,
His drink being seven kinds. At first the infant,
Taking the cordial in the nurse's arms.
And then the whining school-boy with his drop
Or two of porter, just to make him creep
More willingly to school. And then the lover,
Sighing like a furnace o'er his lemonade,
Brewed in whiskey punch. Then a soldier,
Full of strange oaths, and reeling with brandy,
Brutal and beastly, sudden and quick in quarrels,
Seeking the fiend Intemperance,
E'en in the gallows' mouth. And then the justice,
In fair, round belly with madeira lined,
Most elegantly drunk, superbly corned;
Full of wise saws against the use of gin,
And so he swallows wine. The sixth age
Shifts into the dull and bloated rum-drinker;
A spectacle his nose, he's scorched inside;
The wretch's ragged hose a world too wide
For his shrunk limbs; and his once manly hand,
Shaking the cup of tea, well braced with rum,
Seems now five palsied bones. Last drink of all,
That ends intoxication's history,
Is laudanum, self-murder, long oblivion,
Sans faith, sans hope, sans life, sans everything

Old Rye makes a Speech.

I was made to be *eaten*,
And not to be *drank;*
To be thrashed in a barn,
Not soaked in a tank.
I come a as blessing
When put through a *mill;*
As a blight and a curse
When run through a *still.*
Make me up into *loaves,*
And your children are fed;
But if into a *drink,*
I will starve them instead.
In bread I'm a servant,
The eater shall rule;
In drink I am master,
The drinker a fool.
Then remember the warning,
My strength I'll employ:
If eaten, to strengthen;
If drank, to destroy.

Edward Carswell.

The Curse of Alcohol.

God made man in his own image, in the image of God created he him. Who, with impious and polluting hand, defaces the image and superscription of his Maker, and stamps him with the counterfeiting die of the evil one? Alcohol! Man by nature walks erect—lifts his forehead to the stars; power and dominion have been given to him over all the creatures of the earth—he is nature's king.

Who is it that breaks his sceptre of authority, takes from him his imperial crown, and degrades him below the brute? Alcohol! Who destroys his reason, hides her bright beams in mystic clouds that roll around the shattered temple of the soul, curtained in midnight? Alcohol! Who pollutes his heart, and robs it of every noble and generous emotion? Alcohol! Who makes him a madman, and then lashes and halloes on the mad pack of his vilest passions? Who fills our jails with felons, and hangs the trembling wretch on the gallows? Alcohol! Who crowds our almshouses with paupers, our hospitals with disease, and our graveyards with dead? Alcohol!

Do any of you want to be a fool—nay, worse, become the jibe and derision of fools? Let him drink liquor. Do any of you (I care not how proud and virtuous you are)—do any of you want to be a rascal, with a hang-gallows look, or become a low, vulgar vagabond? Drink liquor!

If you are a father, do you want to see your children ragged and ignorant, growing young candidates for the penitentiary and gallows? Drink liquor! If you are a son, and you want to pay with black ingratitude the debt you owe your parents, and bring down their revered gray hairs with sorrow to the grave, *drink liquor!* If you are a husband, and want to steal all the beauty from your wife's face, make her wretched and supremely miserable, *drink liquor!* Do any of you want to lose the property you have gathered together by the sweat of your brow, as a home for your wife and little ones, and a retreat in old age? If so, *drink liquor!* If you want to pay a high premium for being poisoned, *drink liquor!* If you want to bid an eternal farewell to your freedom, and be a greater slave than was ever lashed at night to his dungeon, *drink liquor!* If you want to exchange a healthy body, so "fearfully, wonderfully made," for a disease-cursed frame that a demon would scorn to inhabit and the devil quit in *disgust, drink liquor!* If you want to blast with disease your body from head to heel, sweep every line where manly beauty lingers, and early heap the clay upon a foul mass of corruption more disgusting than the leprosy of Naaman, *drink liquor!* If you want to go to the grave "unhonored and unsung," and let infamy there spread its sable plumes, and fling its blackness o'er a *drunkard's tomb,* drink BODY-BLIGHTING, SPIRIT-BLASTING LIQUOR!

SEVENTY-SIX AND NOW.

OUR sires were rocked in Faneuil Hall,
  The famous cradle of the free;
And shall we hear our brothers call
  For help, and never heed the plea?
We heap the granite to the skies,
  Over the graves on Bunker's Hill;
But if the heroes there could rise,
  While Rum is king, would they be still!

They would again renew their vows,
  To wipe away a nation's stain;
And Warren's thrilling voice would rouse
  The iron will of mighty men.
They would relight their beacon-fires
  On old Wachusett's naked brow,
And clang the bells in all their spires,
  And sow their votes like storms of snow!

Where are the sons of sires who cast
  The taxèd tea-chests in the sea?
Where is the spirit of the past
  That moved the deep of sympathy?

Would not intemperance have been driven
  From us, like a loathsome curse,
If, when our fathers went to heaven,
  Their mantles had been worn by us?

Descendants of the good old stock,
  By all the free blood in your veins,
By all the prayers at Plymouth Rock,
  Strike off the drunkard's galling chains!
By all the blood your fathers shed,
  By all the laurels they have won,
Stand up for Temperance, as they did
  For Liberty at Lexington!

Strike out the statutes which disgrace
  Our land before a wondering world!
Enact a law to lift the race!
  Let vice into its gulf be hurled!
Strike for the glory of our land!
  Strike for the victims bound in chains!
Strike when the heart beats to the hand!
  Strike for the cause the foe disdains!

Go bravely to the ballot-box,
  And cast a freeman's honest vote;
Be never, like the stupid ox,
  Led by the halter at the throat.
Trust not the men who did betray
  Our cause for office, power, or gold;
The promises they make to-day
  They'll break to-morrow, as of old.

Men who make politics a trade,
  Will stoop to-day to tie your shoes;
To-morrow, your cause will be betrayed
  And crucified by bitter foes;

They'll sell it ere the morning dawns,
And nail it to the cursèd tree,
Robe it with scorn, crown it with thorns,
And make of it a mockery.

GEO. W. BUNGAY.

INDICTMENT OF THE TRAFFIC.

IF there be any greater public evil in the land than intemperance, I challenge you to name the monster. Rebellion and treason a few years gone by called for hecatombs of fathers and sons as a sacrifice to the mad ambition of a few men. The victims fell by the thousands. Call the roll of the 300,000 loyal dead, bury them with all honors, write epitaphs, pronounce eulogies, keep green the grass over their heads. They fell in a noble cause. Their dust let all the people honor. But *these*—the poor, besotted, bloated victims of the liquor traffic; these who have been despoiled of manhood, who have died in the gutters of the street or in the chambers of wealth; these who have been made to reek with filth and blasphemy and shame; these in whose bosoms and in whose homes a hell of woes has been set up—count their number. Call the roll of them—call on, you have never done. The list is swelling daily. While you sit here, it is swelling over yonder, and yonder, and yonder—everywhere. This rebellion and treason against human welfare and the general good comes to no end. This war on the lives and souls of men never ceases. They who feed this fire of death are responsible for the flame. The whole traffic is responsible, for the constant tendency and effort of the entire system is to produce all these dire evils. There is nothing counteractive about it. From top to bottom it is temptation, seduction incarnate. Gilded saloons, fancy drinks, grand accommodations, the social glass, affable venders, down through the long chain of agencies, down to the lowest sinks and slums of a great city, all of it from top to bottom is one grand piece of satanic temptation, to unsteady a man's good resolution, to pull him off the throne of self-control, to unman him, to set on fire his passions. From top to bottom the traffic entices the young, holds fast the middle-aged, and, like a vampire, continues to suck the old man's blood so long as he can beg or borrow a penny. The top may get the best blood, the bottom the worst, but the work is one, from the fair beginning to the foul ending. It is a system organized and compacted for human debasement and ruin. It spreads its net-work of death everywhere. It links itself with every amusement, making even the decent dangerous. It hangs about the skirts of all lawful business. It tempts incessantly. It pauses at no expense, for we ourselves pay all its expenses.

My indictment of this monster evil is not half completed. I indict it in the name of all lands and all people, in behalf of all trades and professions, in the name of literature, art, and science, of whom it has ever been the foe. I indict it in behalf of men frozen, men stabbed, men beaten with clubs, men stupefied and burned in fires, men crushed upon railways, men torn by machinery, men eaten to death by its fever, men crowning their life-long misery by suicide. I indict it in the name of helpless griefs, of penniless women and beggared children, of wives who have met a thousand deaths through blasted hopes, agonies of years, ceaseless mortifications. I indict it in the name of religion and in the name of that God who declares a woe to him that putteth the bottle to his neighbor to drink, and who says no drunkard shall inherit the kingdom of heaven. I indict it as a public nuisance and a moral pestilence. And I seem to hear that voice which cursed the old serpent in Eden, speaking again to this demon of modern days, "Because thou hast done this, thou art cursed above all cattle and every beast of the field; upon thy belly shalt thou go, and dust shalt thou eat all the days of thy life." It is idle to deny this responsibility. We array the figures. We show the scars and terrible wounds. We point to the dead, and society may rise, and with a just indignation say to the liquor traffic: "Because thou hast done this."

I summon all the moral reformers and religious teachers of the race, and they all plead against it as the inveterate and deadly foe of all good morals and religion. They point us to men renowned for intellectual magnificence, who by it were degraded to the stupidity and loathsomeness of sots. Every year for generations the state, the ranks of literature, the legal and the medical professions, and the pulpit, have been despoiled of some of their brightest ornaments by this demon. Brilliant lawyers, lofty statesmen, the finest geniuses, distinguished preachers—no one stands too high, no character is too sacred or too pure, to be seized and degraded by this foe of the race.

BELSHAZZAR'S FEAST.

THE king was revelling 'mid his glittering shrines
  His golden goblets had been emptied thrice,
And wasted nectar trickled down in lines
  Upon the table, where he flung his dice.
And great Belshazzar tottered from his throne
  With the intoxication of a king,
And danced before his images of stone,
  And smiled to hear the giddy courtiers sing
Their wanton glee in wild, voluptuous tone.

A thousand lords were feasting in that hall,
  And peerless women sat on every side,
And golden censers swung along the wall,
  And lofty mirrors gleamed with regal pride;
And cups were brought—the sacred cups of old—
  Robbed from the holy Temple of the Lord;
And great Belshazzar drank from one of gold,
  And bade his nobles mock with lance and sword,
And quaff with pride and profanation bold.

The lords polluted with their vicious hands
  The sacred cups, and boasted of their power,
And offered incense to their idol bands—
  Alas! for them. It was an evil hour,
For suddenly appeared before them all
  An apparition, chilling with affright—
A livid hand loomed out above the ball,
  The chandeliers ceased shedding forth their light,
And high that hand wrote fire upon the wall.

Aghast, Belshazzar called soothsayers in
  To tell the meaning of that living line—
Oh! "MENE, MENE, TEKEL, UPHARSIN:'
  Woe to Chaldea—these are words divine;
But they knew not the mystery which they read,
  And sent for Daniel to interpret it.
"Thou art found wanting, king," the prophet said,
  "Thy mighty sceptre hath Jehovah split;
A Mede shall rule this night when thou art dead."

But great Belshazzar sought again his wine,
  And, though he shook before the holy seer,
Still rolled upon his purple couch supine,
  And drank the more to quench his guilty fear.

That night, while giddy pleasure held her reign,
  A Persian foe stood at the monarch's gate;
Their host turned broad Euphrates from her lane,
  The sword of Cyrus sealed Chaldea's fate,
And ere the morn was great Belshazzar slain.

EDWIN POCOCKE.

A TEETOTALER—WHY?

WHY am I a teetotaler? you ask, and I reply,
If any one should be so, why also should not I?
If duty sounds her call, should I not eager be,
A soldier of the right, to prove my loyalty?
If there be good to get, more good may be my share;
If there be good to give, to give should be my care.
I know the evil wrought—nay, not a soul on earth
Knows half the sin and woe to which strong drink gives birth.
If that dark woe and sin can by my help be made
Of all its sable hues to lose the smallest shade;
Or if my word and deed may shelter some,
By blessing of our God, from darker doom to come,
I spurn all thought of taste and fashion's coaxing plea,
And as a firm teetotaler I proudly mean to be.
If I touch not strong drink, no stain is on my soul
From bloodshed or foul crime caused by the toxic bowl;
This root of thousand plagues I nothing do to nurse,
But try my best to rid the world from this great curse.
Oh! sweetest comfort this. And then my prayer can fly
Unweighted and unchecked beyond the sky,
That snares may be removed, temptations cease to slay,
Man's cruelest betrayers for ever speed away,

And Christ's own kingdom come in glory and in might,
The joy of highest heaven, and earth's supreme delight.
Why am I a teetotaler? you ask, and I reply,
I'm honest man and patriot, and *Christian; that* is why.
And, questioners, if you the answer will pursue,
What I for long have done, *you* will begin to do!

REV. D. BURNS, A.M.

THE TRUE REMEDY.

WITH this gigantic evil confronting us, the question which presses upon every Christian conscience is this: What is the remedy? How are we to meet it? Now, we think that we have got the very best remedy, the sure and only remedy, in total abstinence. There are some things about that which I would like to say, albeit they may be very simple and elementary, yet it is sometimes very beneficial to go down to first principles. This abstinence is dangerous to none; it will injure no one's health; it is safe for all; it is expedient, too, for all. If there be two courses of conduct, one of which is attended with danger, and the other attended with none, prudence says that the safe course ought to be taken and the dangerous one avoided. But this argument, applied to the case in hand, will lead directly to abstinence. There is moderation, so-called; and there is abstinence. There is danger in the one, but there is none in the other; therefore the course of abstinence ought to be pursued. The only way in which you can meet that argument is to say that there is no danger in moderation; but who is there that will take such a stand as that in the face of the facts which are staring at us from every street-corner. No danger in the moderate use of intoxicating liquor! Why, how many who have begun in moderation have ended in helpless intemperance! And how is the danger in these days increased by the injurious and pernicious customs which prevail in social life! How many who began in manhood, hopeful and apparently well, have been ensnared by those terrible customs, and are now, to all human appearance, entirely ruined! And that which has been with them may be with us also. "Let him that thinketh he standeth take heed lest he fall."

This cause of abstinence is necessary for the drunkard. I agree thoroughly with all that has been said already in declaring intemperance a crime; but wherever it has become a habit with a man, it is also a physical disease, so that we must look at that side of the matter too, and attempt to grapple with it. He who continually indulges in strong drink till he acquires the habit of drunkenness becomes physically diseased, so that his stomach is affected by the least drop of alcohol that enters into it, and becomes inflamed with the desire for more. Hence, for the drunkard, abstinence is his only hope. But this being so, we immediately make our appeal to others, and say, "Are you going to let him abstain alone?" There are many men who would rather go down into a drunkard's grave than be pointed at and have it said regarding them that they needed to be abstainers in order to save themselves from intemperance. How can we prevent them from feeling this humiliation? Only by those of us who have never lain under any imputation of intemperance taking our stand beside them, and saying: "We will support you in the position which you take, and who accus or attacks you accuses or attacks us." There is sympathy in this, and it is the power of sympathy which most touches the heart for cure. The general has most power with his troops when, putting himself at their head, he says, "Come, follow me"; and we shall have most power with the drunkard when we put ourselves beside him, and say, "Two are better than one, for, if one fall, his neighbor can help him up."

REV. WM. M. TAYLOR.

THE WRECKERS.

HARK! to the roar of the surges,
Hark! to the wild winds' howl;
See the black cloud that the hurricane urges
Bend like a maniac's scowl!
Full on the sunken lee ledges
Laps the devoted bark;
And the loud waves, like a hundred sledges,
Smite to the doomèd mark!

Shrilly the shriek of the seaman
Cleaves like a dart through the roar;
Harsh as the pitiless laugh of a demon
Rattles the pebbled shore.
Ho! for the life-boat, brothers;
Now may the hearts of the brave,
Hurling their lives to the rescue of others,
Conquer the stormy wave.

Shame for humanity's treason!
Shame for the form we wear!
Blush at the temple of pity and reason
Turned to a robber's lair!
Worse than the horrible breakers,
Worse than the shattering storm,
See the rough-handed, remorseless wreckers
Stripping the clay yet warm.

Plucking at girlhood's tresses,
Tangled with gems and gold;
Snatching love-tokens from manhood's caresses,
Clenched with a dying hold.
What of the shrieks of despairing?
What of the last faint gasp?
Robbers, who lived would but lessen your sharing:
Gold—'twas a god in your grasp!

Boys in their sunny brown beauty,
Men in their rugged bronze,
Women whose wail might have taught wolves a duty,
Dead on the merciless stones.
Tenderly slid o'er the plundered
Shrouds from the white-capped surge;
Loud on the traitors the mad ocean thundered—
Low o'er the lost sang a dirge.

Wo! there are deadlier breakers,
Billows that burn as they roll!
Flanked by a legion of crueler wreckers—
Wreckers of body and soul;
Traitors to God and humanity,
Circes that hold in their arms
Blood-dripping murder and hopeless insanity,
Folly and famine by turns.

Crested with wine redly flashing,
Swollen with liquid fire,
How the strong ruin comes fearfully dashing,
High as the soul walks, and higher!
Virtue, and manhood, and beauty,
Hope and the sunny-haired bliss,
With the diviner white angel of duty,
Sink in the burning abyss.

What if the soul of the drunkard
Shrivel in quenchless flame?
What though his children, by beggary conquered,
Plunge into ruin and shame?
Gold has come in to the wreckers,
Murder has taken his prize;
Gold, though a million hearts burst on the breakers,
Smothers the crime and the cries!

C. C. BURLEIGH.

WOMAN'S WORK.

WOMEN, there are some things that you can do, and this is one: you can make drinking unpopular and disgraceful among the young. You can utterly discountenance all drinking in your own house, and you can hold in suspicion every young man who touches the cup. You know that no young man who drinks can safely be trusted with the happiness of any woman, and that he is as unfit as a man can be for a woman's society. Have this understood—that every young man who drinks is socially proscribed. Bring up your children to regard drinking as not only dangerous, but disgraceful. Place temptation in no man's way. If men will make beasts of themselves, let them do it in other society than yours. Recognize the living terrible fact that wine has always been, and is to-day, the curse of your sex; that it steals the hearts of men away from you, that it dries up your prosperity, that it endangers your safety, that it can only bring you evil. If social custom compels you to present wine at your feasts, rebel against it, and make a social custom in the interests of virtue and purity. The matter is very much in your own hands. The women of the country, in what is called polite society, can do more to make the nation temperate than all the legislators and tumultuous reformers that are struggling and blundering in their efforts to this end.

A Boast of King Bacchus.

I AM a mighty king, second to none!
Men bow before me, acknowledge me lord!
I am a mighty king; thousands I sway,
Laugh at their folly, plunge them in Hades;
Mine are the purple grapes; mine the hot juice;
Mine are the sunny slopes laden with vines;
Mine are the orchards, with juicy fruits rich;
Mine are the hop-grounds; they are my power;
Mine are the barley-fields, waving with grain.
I am a mighty king, second to none;
Men bow before me, acknowledge me lord!
I am their master; I lay them low,
Wither their manhood, deep plunge them in Hades.
Mine is the ivy crown, glossy and green;
Mine is the golden cup, brimming with wine;
Mine is the crimson flood, fiery and hot;
I in it plunge my slaves, drown them in wine,
Laugh at their folly, consign them to Hades!
Mine is the scarlet cloak, mine the wild goat;
Mine is the stormy heart—tears never melt it;
Mine is the stern will—man bows before it.
For I am a great king; thousands I sway;
The earth is my throne, souls are my prey.
Kings fall before me, empires I rend;
Home-ties I sever, gray hairs bow to death.
I reason scorn; mockingly pledge him:
He is my foe; I do not fear him!
Mock his wise sermons, point to my prey!
I quaff the red wine; my heart it grows bold.

I wildly revel; smile on the widow,
Whisper, "I slew him; I in Hades hurled him!
His soul I destroyed!" laugh at her tears.
For I am a great king, second to none!
Men bow before me; they are my slaves!
I the wife's fairest hopes mock and destroy;
Point to my slave; whisper, "He's mine!"
Vain are his efforts; I crush her through him!
I to the grave doom her, laugh as she dies!
I fill the wine-cup; drink to my triumph!
For man is my slave; I am his master.
I make the old mother's tears to flow;
Laugh at her anguish; show her her boy—
In mad revel show him; show him in death!
I mock the father's woe: "*Is this thy boy?*"
Give him the wine-cup, drug him for Hades,
Laugh as he wildly raves, mock him with hope.
He cursing dies; I in triumph laugh!
I make the orphans, I to death give them;
I in sin rear them, in darkest shades hurl them!
I am a mighty king; man is my slave!
Men bow before me, drink to their master.
They seize the brimming bowl—gladly I give!
Man is my slave; he bows before me,
Prays for my favors, lives for my gifts.
Him I befriend, with my heel on his neck;
Low in dust hold; give him the wine-cup!
He my hand kisses; grovels before me;
I in my grasp hold him—he cannot fly!
I into shades of darkest night hurl him,
Kill him with steel, drown him in ocean,
Bid him strike boldly home, bid him be brave;
For I am his master, he is my slave.

Opposite Examples.

I ASK the young man who is just forming his habits of life, or just beginning to indulge those habitual trains of thought out of which habits grow, to look round him, and mark the examples whose fortune he would covet or whose fate he would abhor. Even as we walk the streets we meet with exhibitions of each extreme. Here behold a patriarch whose stock of vigor three-score years and ten seem hardly to have impaired. His erect form, his firm step, his elastic limbs, and undimmed senses are so many certificates of good conduct. His fair complexion shows that his blood has never been corrupted ; his pure breath, that he has never yielded his digestive apparatus to abuse ; his exact language and keen apprehension, that his brain has never been drugged or stupefied by the poisons of distiller or tobacconist. Enjoying his appetites to the highest, he has preserved the power of enjoying them. As he drains the cup of life, there are no lees at the bottom. His organs will reach the goal of existence together. Painlessly as a candle burns down in its socket, so will he expire.

But look at an opposite extreme, where an opposite history is recorded. What wreck so shocking to behold as the wreck of a dissolute man ; the vigor of life exhausted, and yet the first steps in an honorable career not taken ; in himself a lazar-house of disease ; dead, but, by a heathenish custom of society, not buried ! Rogues have had the initial letter of their title burnt into the palms of their hands, even for murder. Cain was only branded on the forehead ; but over the whole person of the debauchee or the inebriate the signatures of infamy are written. How nature brands him with stigma and opprobrium ! How she hangs labels all over him, to testify her disgust at his existence, and to admonish others to beware of his example! How she loosens all his joints, sends tremors along his muscles, and bends forward his frame, as if to bring him upon all fours with kindred brutes, or to degrade him to the reptiles crawling! How she disfigures his countenance, as if intent upon obliterating all traces of her own image, so that she may swear she never made him! How she pours rheum over his eyes, sends foul spirits to inhabit his breath, and shrieks as with a trumpet, from every pore of his body, "*Behold a beast!*" Such a man may be seen in the streets of our cities every day; if rich enough, he may be found in the saloons and at the tables of the "upper ten"; but surely to every man of purity and honor, to every man whose wisdom as well as whose heart is unblemished, the wretch who comes cropped and bleeding from the pillory, and redolent with its appropriate perfumes, would be a guest or a companion far less offensive and disgusting.

Now let the young man, rejoicing in his manly proportions and in his comeliness, look on this picture, and on this, and then say after the likeness of which he intends his own erect stature and sublime countenance shall be configured.

HORACE MANN.

MEN WANTED.

THE world wants men—large-hearted, manly men;
Men who shall join its chorus, and prolong
The psalm of labor and the psalm of love.
The times want scholars—scholars who shall shape
The doubtful destinies of dubious years,
And land the ark that bears our country's good
Safe on some peaceful Ararat at last.
The age wants heroes—heroes who shall dare
To struggle in the solid ranks of truth;

To clutch the monster error by the throat;
To bear opinion to a loftier seat;
To blot the era of oppression out,
And lead a universal freedom in.
And heaven wants souls—fresh and capacious souls;
To taste its raptures, and expand, like flowers,
Beneath the glory of its central sun.
It wants fresh souls—not lean and shrivelled ones;
It wants fresh souls. My brother, give it thine.
If thou indeed wilt be what scholars should;
If thou wilt be a hero, and wilt strive
To help thy fellow and exalt thyself,
Thy feet, at last, shall stand on jasper floors;
Thy heart, at last, shall seem a thousand hearts—
Each single heart with myriad raptures filled—
While thou shalt sit with princes and with kings,
Rich in the jewel of a ransomed soul.

LICENSE OR NO LICENSE? "THAT'S THE QUESTION."

THE question rises to a people's eye,
Shall we still wear the tyrant's galling chain,
Obey a demon that shall crush our souls?
Shall this proud land still wear the garb of vice?
Shall guilt be legalized, and exiled peace?
Shall men be brutalized, and fond hearts crushed?
Shall wisdom stride insulted from our arms?
Shall virtue look in pity and contempt
Upon the creatures who have spurned her boons?
Shall poison be the traffic of our day?
Shall health and life be sacrificed to vice?
Shall homes be rendered desolate and sad?
Shall doting spirits see their idols slain?

The fair hopes of a lifetime crushed in shame,
The pride of youth laid low within the grave—
Shall this be so? Shall that strong shield, the law,
Be made the instrument of such a work?
Forbid it, citizens! Your own proud rights
Command the wielding of that privilege
To drive the demon from your very hearth,
To strip him of his fangs, and bid him die!
'Tis yours to rescue now your fellow-men
From death—the worst he may endure or know—
The double death of body and of soul!
And 'tis within your midst—'tis no wild dream,
No phantom of the fancy that we paint!
Our youth have tasted, and, by wine beguiled,
Have wandered down the path of guilt and vice,
Till e'en the gray hairs of their sires have bowed
Beneath the weight of their own children's sin!
The fairest of our noble land have sunk
Beneath the simoon that hath swept it o'er!
It cometh like a thief, yet, in its strength.
'Tis as destruction's besom all aroused!
Spirits of gentle and sweet purity
Have shrunk and withered 'neath its blighting touch;
Young hearts have seen their dear ones stricken down,
Have felt their all of happiness decay,
Scathed by this demon's blow!
Fame's laurel wreath
Hath lost its bloom, and fallen from the brow
Of many a soul whose manly efforts there
Had wasted life's bright energies to win
That very wreath, which now they careless spurn!
All this hath this vile monster done, and more!
He hath robbed infants in their helplessness
Of childhood's only stay! He hath deprived
The feebler mother of her every power;
Hath stolen from her bosom's shrine that heart
For which she would have sacrificed her all!

He hath torn down the barrier between
The brute creation and God's image, man!
Hath laid the soul immortal in the dust,
And taught it longings grovelling as the swine!
Hath quenched ambition's spirit-stirring flame—
Hath driven from out the inmost soul the life
That savored full of immortality!
Hath hastened to the victim's couch the form
Of its grim sister, Death!
                                        Hath rent the soul
Till e'en the heart-strings quiver, while fair hope
Hath fled, unwilling exile, from its shrine!
This have we seen, and in our very midst—
Beside the hearth-stones sacred to our souls,
Among the loved ones cherished proudly there!
And when the weapon's placed within our hand
Shall we not ward the monster's blow, and strive
To rid our altars of its blasting breath?
Oh! let THIS PEOPLE'S mighty voice reply,
"*The victory shall be ours*—WE WILL BE FREE!"

TEMPERANCE VINDICATOR.

THE PLEDGE! THE PLEDGE!

Give us the pledge! Why do you object? Is it because you love the stimulus—the alcohol! Then you are in danger, and for your own sake you ought to sign it. No man can have a fondness for the excitement or the stimulus of alcoholic drinks without being in danger of becoming a drunkard. Do you feel at certain regular times a periodical craving for "a drink," whether before breakfast, at eleven o'clock, or just before dinner? If you do, *beware!* you are in *great danger!* 'Tis an appetite "that grows by what it feeds on." Do you feel that "you want bracing"? Then *beware!* The stomach of no healthy man wants "bracing," and if you resort to *drink* for that purpose, be sure that you have drunk too often and too much. It is drinking—unnatural, unwholesome, *alcoholic drinking*—which causes that morbid state of the nerves and the stomach that makes you feel that "aching void." It is the best possible evidence that you have gone too far, and that you must stop short or be ruined.

But again we say, Give us the pledge! Do you say, "I am a perfectly sober man, and never drink, and therefore do not require the aid of the pledge"? Be it so. But are you not a husband or a father; a son or a brother, an uncle or a nephew; a relative or a friend even? Are you not a MAN? Are you not a member of society? Are you totally isolated in the world? Is your example of no value whatever? Are you so totally insignificant that you are of no consequence whatever in society? It is not and it cannot be so. No man is so utterly wretched and valueless. Suppose you have a son who is in danger of falling; suppose that he does fall; and in reply to your lamentations or reproaches he should say, "Father, I would have signed the pledge, and I would have kept it, had you set me the example; but you declined it; I but follow your example, and you must share the responsibility." Would not your mouth be shut? Would not those words sear your heart as with a hot iron?

Again we say, Sign the pledge, and you will have done your duty, and that duty is not performed until you have done it.

How Jamie came Home.

Come, mother, set the kettle on,
And put the ham and eggs to fry—
Something to eat,
And make it neat,
To please our Jamie's mouth and eye;
For Jamie is our only son, you know—
The rest have perished long ago!
He's coming from the wars to-night,
And his blue eyes will sparkle bright,
And his old smile will play right free,
His old, loved home again to see.

I say for 't! 'twas a cur'us thing
That Jamie was not maimed or killed!
Five were the years,
With hopes and fears,
And gloomy, hopeless tidings filled;
And many a night, the past five years,
We've lain within our cottage here,
And, while the rain-storm came and went,
We've thought of Jamie in his tent,
And offered many a silent prayer,
That God would keep him in his care.

I say for 't! *'twas* a cur'us thing
That Jamie was not maimed or killed!
Five were the years,
With blood and tears,
With cruel, bloody battles filled;
And many a morn, the past five years,
We've knelt around our fireside here,
And while we thought of bleeding ones,
Our blazing towns and smoking guns,
We've thought of him, and breathed a prayer
That God would keep him in his care.

And he shall tell us of his fights,
His marches, skirmishes, and all;
Many a tale
Will make us pale,
And pity those who had to fall;
And many a tale of sportive style
Will go, perhaps, to make us smile;
And when his stories all are done,
And when the evening well has gone,
We'll kneel around the hearth once more,
And thank the Lord the war is o'er.

Hark! there's a sound! he's coming now;
Hark! mother! there's the sound once more;
Now on our feet,
With smiles to greet,
We'll meet him at the opening door!
It is a heavy step and tone—
Too heavy, far, for one alone;
Perhaps the company extends
To some of his old army friends;
And who they be, and whence they came,
Of course we'll welcome them the same.

What bear ye on your shoulders, men?
Is it my Jamie, stark and dead?
What did you say?
Once more, I pray—
I did not gather what you said.
What! *drunk!* you tell that LIE to me?
What! DRUNK! O God! it cannot be!
It cannot be my Jamie dear
Lying in drunken slumber here!
It is, it is, as you have said!
Men, lay him on yon waiting bed.

'Tis Jamie, yes! a bearded man,
  Though bearing still some boyhood's trace;
      Stained with the ways
      Of reckless days,
  Flushed with the wine-cup in his face;
Swelled with the fruits of reckless years,
Robbed of each trait that e'er endears,
Except the heart-distressing one
That Jamie is our only son.

O mother! take the kettle off,
  And set the ham and eggs away!
      What was my crime,
      And when the time,
  That I should live to see this day?
For all the sighs I ever drew,
And all the grief I ever knew,
And all the tears I ever shed
Above our children that are dead,
And all the care that creased my brow,
Were naught to what comes o'er me now.

I would to God that when the three
  We lost were hidden from our view,
      Jamie had died,
      And by their side
  Had lain all pure and spotless too!
I would this rain might fall above
The grave of him we joyed to love,
Rather than hear its coming traced
Upon this roof he has disgraced!
But, mother, Addie, come this way,
And let us kneel, and humbly pray.

WILL M. CARLETON.

WHAT IS THE LIQUOR-SHOP?

A VAMPIRE fattening on the pain
Of bleeding hearts and children slain;
A foe to virtue, learning, truth,
The bane of age and snare of youth;
A licensed woe and murder den,
A curse and pest to honest men;
A nation's burning blot and shame,
Which all its noblest deeds defame;
Death's gilded door, round which men wait,
And madly take the poisoned bait;
A source from which pollution streams,
Darkening beauty's heavenly beams;
The poor man's foe and wise man's dread,
Where poverty to vice is wed;
A trumpet-call to all the good
To join in holy brotherhood
This glaring wrong to sweep away,
And hydra hosts of evil slay;
The misery and crime it brings
To rank among departed things,
Whose spectres, trembling in the gloom,
Us wakeful keep, lest it resume
Its blasted sway, and, daring, wage
Destructive warfare with the age.
Then rouse ye, all who hold the helm
Of public action in the realm!
Mark well the facts within your reach,
For these a fearful lesson teach
Of fostering ignorance and sin
In these abodes of beer and gin.
If, then, from guilt you would be free,
Declare this evil shall not be!

Introductory.

A HAPPY greeting for all. We welcome parents and friends to another meeting. If you look around, you see that our faces are glad. Why do we look glad? It is because we *are* glad!

"We're glad we're in this army"—the Temperance Army! We are glad of the approval which so many parents and friends are giving to our efforts. It is to us like the clear sunshine of spring. We are glad for what we expect to enjoy at this meeting. We have songs prepared, and recitations, declamations, and dialogues. Prayer will be offered, and we expect a short address from our minister or some one else at the close. We are glad to have a temperance society of our own. We feel that it is good to pledge ourselves against intoxicating drinks, profanity, and tobacco. We enjoy voting for our own officers. We like to get new members. We are trying to get every boy and girl in the place. We like to speak and to hear our mates speak. We enjoy the dialogues and the commendations we sometimes get from our ministers and parents and others.

Some folks may say, "It is small business—nothing but children's play." Well, we guess the world would be a dreary place without some children's play; and the best of it is that our *play* here is good *work*, and our *work* here is good *play*. Our work here is good play for us, because we like it so well; and our *play* here is good *work*, because we learn to remember, to think, to speak, to hate drinking, swearing, and smoking, and to love the temperance cause and every other good cause. But we are sure *you* will not call our little steps toward a good future child's play. If the steps are *small*, the day of *small* things should not be despised. We are glad you have come to see us trip playfully along our ways of pleasantness. We renew our happy greeting, and hope you will approve and enjoy our songs and recitations and dialogues, and the collection too.

THE TEMPERANCE GIANT.

I AM strong in contention; ay, strong in my wrath;
Through the mountain and valley I've hewn out a path;
And wherever I go,
Be it swiftly or slow,
I shall strike down the foemen of truth with a blow.
I say to the rocks, Ye shall burst with despair
As my way to the future ye haste to prepare;
While out of the forest I summon the trees
To make me a jacket to wear on the seas.
They come at my bidding, and grant my behest,
For they know it is useless my way to arrest.
From nothing I shrink;
And what do you think?
I only want plenty of water to drink!

My sinews are iron, my nerves are of steel,
The savage invader I crush 'neath my heel;
I grind at the mill,
And never am still,
Yet always I whistle with cheery good-will,
If those who would use me don't seek to abuse,
And give me more food than I know how to use;
But if they neglect me, the penalty's sure—
A good blowing-up they will have to endure!

It is no easy thing for a giant, you know,
To get up his steam and determine to go;
And once under way,
It is work, and not play,
For the spirit within him he's bound to obey!

The giants are many that traverse the earth,
With light and with darkness they sprang into birth;
And as onward they go,
Be it swiftly or slow,
Some good they will take, or some good they'll bestow.
Some blight with their touch the sweet blossoms that grace
Our homes, and so foully their beauty deface
That we turn with a shudder whenever their breath
Is nigh, for we know 'tis the savor of death!
Intemperate demons are these who destroy
The altars of peace and the fountains of joy.
From such let us shrink
With abhorrence, and think
It is something much stronger than water they drink.

More temperance giants our country requires
To manage its work and to kindle its fires—
Strong men who'll engage
Strong warfare to wage
Against the great curse of this rum-ridden age!
At the desk, at the counter, in halls of debate,
If high his position or low his estate,
A man we would find, uncorrupted by pelf,
A law to his neighbor, a law to himself!
Go, count up the terrible deeds you have known,
And marvel why men can't let whiskey alone,
When so low they can sink.
Oh! shouldn't you think
That they'd rather have water, pure water, to drink?

JOSEPHINE POLLARD.

THE LIQUOR INTEREST.

TRAMP, tramp, tramp, the boys are marching; how many of them? Sixty thousand! Sixty full regiments, every man of which will, before twelve months shall have completed their course, lie down in the grave of a drunkard! Every year during the past decade has witnessed the same sacrifice; and, sixty regiments stand behind this army ready to take its place. It is to be recruited from our children and our children's children. "Tramp, tramp, tramp"—the sounds come to us in the echoes of the footsteps of the army just expired; tramp, tramp, tramp—the earth shakes with the tread of the host now passing; tramp, tramp, tramp, comes to us from the camp of the recruits. A great tide of life flows resistlessly to its death. What in God's name are they fighting for? The privilege of pleasing an appetite, of conforming to a social usage, of filling sixty thousand homes with shame and sorrow, of loading the public with the burden of pauperism, of crowding our prison-houses with felons, of detracting from the productive industries of the country, of ruining fortunes and breaking hopes, of breeding disease and wretchedness, of destroying both body and soul in hell before their time.

The prosperity of the liquor interest, covering every department of it, depends entirely on the maintenance of this army. It cannot live without it. It never did live without it. So long as the liquor interest maintains its present prosperous condition, it will cost America the sacrifice of sixty thousand men every year. The effect is inseparable from the cause. The cost to the country of the liquor traffic is a sum so stupendous that any figures which we should dare to give would convict us of trifling. The amount of life absolutely destroyed, the amount of industry sacrificed, the amount of bread transformed into poison, the shame, the unavailing sorrow, the crime, the poverty, the pauperism, the brutality, the wild waste of vital and financial resources, make an aggregate so vast, so incalculably vast, that the only wonder is that the American people do not rise as one man, and declare that this great curse shall exist no longer. Dilettante conventions are held on the subject of peace by men and women who find it necessary to fiddle to keep themselves awake. A hue-and-cry is raised about woman suffrage, as if any wrong which may be involved in woman's lack of the suffrage could be compared to the wrongs attached to the liquor interest

Does any sane woman doubt that women are suffering a thousand times more from rum than from any political disability?

The truth is that there is no question before the American people to-day that begins to match in importance the temperance question. The question of American slavery was never anything but a baby by the side of this; and we prophesy that within ten years, if not within five, the whole country will be awake to it and divided upon it. The organizations of the liquor interest, the vast funds at its command, the universal feeling among those whose business is pitted against the national prosperity and the public morals — these are enough to show that, upon one side of this matter, at least, the present condition of things and the social and political questions that lie in the immediate future are apprehended. The liquor interest knows there is to be a great struggle, and is preparing to meet it. People both in this country and in Great Britain are beginning to see the enormity of this business—are beginning to realize that Christian civilization is actually poisoned at its fountain, and that there can be no purification of it until the source of the poison is dried up.

Meantime, the tramp, tramp, tramp sounds on — the

tramp of sixty thousand yearly victims. Some are besotted and stupid; some are wild with hilarity, and dance along the dusty way; some reel along in pitiful weakness; some wreak their mad and murderous impulses on one another, or on the helpless women and children whose destinies are united to theirs; some stop in wayside debaucheries and infamies for a moment; some go bound in chains, from which they seek in vain to wrench their bleeding wrists; and all are poisoned in body and soul, and all are doomed to death. Wherever they move, crime, poverty, shame, wretchedness, and despair hover in awful shadows. There is no bright side to the picture. We forget: there is just one. The men who make this army get rich. Their children are robed in purple and fine linen, and live upon dainties. Some of them are regarded as respectable members of society, and they hold conventions to protect their interests! Still the tramp, tramp, tramp goes on.—J. G. HOLLAND, *in Scribner's Monthly.*

NO DRUNKARD IN HEAVEN.

No drunkard in heaven! there temperance reigns,
And no reeling inebriate o'er the bright plains
Will stumble, and totter, and fall by the way,
As if night had usurped the glad sceptre of day.

No drunkard in heaven! each eye is as clear
As if never on earth was it dimmed by a tear,
And calmly and steadily looks on the light
Which showeth God's glory to man's renewed sight.

No drunkard in heaven! each heart is awake,
The bliss of the seraphs and saints to partake,

To share in the joy of that all-perfect love,
Uniting pure hearts in the mansions above.

No drunkard in heaven! oh! if thou wouldst be
A lone, drifting wreck on eternity's sea,
Fill high the red bowl, and thy libations pour
To the Bacchus who wasteth the soul evermore.

No drunkard in heaven! oh! pause in thy path,
Ere the cloud which is gath'ring around thee in wrath,
Shall its fury expend on thy shelterless head,
And its red bolts of justice be faithfully sped.

No drunkard in heaven! yet mayst thou be there,
To greet the dear friends that white raiment shall wear,
To bless the kind hand which the pledge offered thee,
And the power that hath helped thee through it to be
free!

REV. PHEBE A. HANAFORD, *in Temp. Album.*

NECESSITY OF PERSEVERANCE.

WE must not grow weary in well-doing. The cause of temperance is the cause of Christ, and sooner or later will surely triumph. The true soldier fights from principle and for principle. He would rather die a score of deaths than deserve the reputation of a coward. In this moral warfare we should be true soldiers. We know not how soon our cause will triumph; for it is none of our business to know. We know this, and that is enough to nerve us to our greatest and best efforts: that our cause is right, and, being right, will ultimately win the field. This is as certain as that Christ shall reign until he hath put all enemies under his feet. Intemperance is one of those enemies, and must go down before he shall give up the kingdom to the Father.

The perseverance necessary to sustain the vigorous and protracted efforts that must still be put forth in the cause of temperance will require the strength and inspiration of the Christian faith. We fear that anything short of this will give way before the ever-recurring difficulties that will arise, and the constantly-increasing sacrifices that will be required. The leaders especially must be men of this faith, and, with the needful enthusiasm in their own hearts, they should be able to arouse the same in the hearts of others. The boldest of the ancient prophets was sometimes despondent; but the word of the Lord would revive the spirit of his mind, and Elijah was himself again. If this prophet of God in his Master's cause needed divine assurance and inspiration, how much more do the leading prophets in this moral reform need a similar support? They must meet and overcome present discouragements by looking to the same Source of strength.

A true friend continues faithful to us in our adversity. He feels more and works harder for us in our reverses than when all things go well with us. That will be a marked characteristic in every true friend of temperance. The more his services are needed, the more promptly and cheerfully will they be offered and devoted to the cause. Let every one work on with unceasing, increasing zeal, looking only to the righteousness of the cause, the true sources of wisdom and strength, and the blessed effects upon the character of the laborer of invincible fidelity to high and worthy principle.

REV. N. E. COBLEIGH.

Let every Vote be No.

VOTE yes! and the lava-tide of death
  Over cottage, hall, and bower
Shall roll its dark, blood-crested wave,
  While madness rules the hour.

Vote no! and the white-winged angel, Peace,
  Shall dwell in the drunkard's home;
And beams of temperance, truth, and light
  Dispel the withering gloom.

Vote yes! and the careworn heart will break,
  The pale lip hush its prayer;
The wretched drunkard downward haste
  To realms of dark despair.

Vote no! and the mother's heart will leap,
  The sister's eye be dry,
The poor inebriate clasp his hands,
  And raise his voice on high.

Oh! then, by the life which God hath given,
  By your powers to curse or bless,
By your fears of hell and your hope of heaven,
  Let not your vote be yes.

By the cherished heart's bitter wrong,
  By the spirit's deathless woe—
In the name of God and the name of man,
  Let every vote be no.

INTEMPERANCE THE GREAT SOCIAL BATTLE OF THE AGE.

THIS is the great social battle of the age which we are fighting between the flesh and the spirit—between the animal and the man. We are living in a time when nothing can save us but moral principle in the individual. Our government is an equal government, as such. We have cast in our destiny on this great principle of popular government, and we must go up with it, or go down with it. It is for us to maintain our institutions, if they are maintained at all; and unless we can teach individuals and the masses self-respect and self-control, we are utterly ruined. It is a mere matter of time. There is no salvation for institutions like ours except in the principle of self-control. And there is no single evil, social or political, that strikes more at the foundation of such institutions than the drinking habits of society. If you corrupt the working-class by drink; if you corrupt the great middle-class by drink; if you corrupt the literary and wealthy classes by drink, you have destroyed the commonwealth beyond your power to save it. And we are making battle for the preservation of this moral principle. It is the great patriotic movement of the day. Therefore we must have clear heads; we must have right consciences; we must have all the manhood that is in men, or that can educate them to it. The good that is in society will not be a match for the evil that is continually pulling it down.

Now, young men, which side are you to take in this great struggle? Will you go for license? Will you go for passion? Will you go for corruption? Or will you range yourselves on the side of those who are attempting to lift men up toward spirituality; toward true reason; toward noble self-control? You can afford to go but one way. Every young man who has one impulse of heroism, one generous tendency in him, ought in the beginning to take his ground beyond all controversy, and say, "I work for those who work for the good and beautiful and true."

HENRY WARD BEECHER.

TAKE A STAND.

IF temperance men would take a stand,
  And show their true position,
Nor yield a point to friend or foe,
  Or scheming politician;
If they would fight for principle,
  For justice and for right,
And whatsoe'er they find to do,
  Would do it with their might,
Our land, which now is so corrupt
  That all good men abhor it,
Might lift her trailing banner up,
  And be the better for it.

If those for whom we cast our vote
  Would not so oft betray us,
And, weakly shrinking from their trust,
  On error's side array us;
If they would only bravely stand
  And face the wily foe,
And in each point of right or wrong
  Say firmly yes or no,
Our land, which now is so corrupt
  That all good men abhor it,
Might lift her trailing banner up,
  And surely be better for it.

CHRISTIAN STATESMAN.

The Bards of Bacchus.

THEY may sing of the joys in the wine-cup that dwell,
And in music the raptures of drunkenness tell,
And over the filth of debauchery throw
The splendors of genius to cover their woe;
Believe not their tale, nor the falsehood repeat,
Though the lie be in verse, and its music most sweet.
From the song that's inspired by a bottle of wine,
Though 'tis sung by love's lips, turn away, brother mine.

Do they think, when they babble of pleasures that spring
From the vintage-crowned bowl, that we know not the sting
Of the serpent that hides in the beaker, though bright
Is the sparkle that plays round its brim, like the light?
Do they tell of the fevers, the headaches, that, born
Of the midnight's excess, crown the debauchee's morn?
Of the pockets collapsed, of the rubicund nose,
Of the rheum in the eyes, and the gout in the toes?

Not they, precious souls! It would ruin their verse!
And why should they make what is bad enough worse?
It would turn topsy-turvy a cart-load of rhyme,
And convict them of *sense*, which, in such bards, is a *crime*.
Lewd songs and lewd singing, alas! would be o'er,
Nor gin-guzzling Byron nor wine-bibbing Moore
Be held up as patterns by bardlings who think
That the fountain of song is a can of strong drink.

Let them sing what they list, let them live as they will,
And worship old Bacchus, and guzzle his swill;

And dream, if they can, that the joy which they find
In the madd'ning debauch is a balm to the mind.
They may cheat their own souls with their songs and
their lies,
But the boys of the PLEDGE, they have ears and have
eyes;
By the wine-cup untempted *their* song shall still be,
"THE FOUNTAIN SHALL FURNISH THE DRINK OF THE
FREE!"

WILLIAM H. BURLEIGH.

THE SLUGGARD, THE BEAST, AND THE DRUNKARD.

THE drunkard drinks until he has drunk all the money out of his purse, all the sense out of his head, all the honor out of his character, and then there is no difference between him and the beast. Yes, begging the beast's pardon, there *is* a difference. The beast can go forward and keep its way. The beast has not abused its own nature; has not degraded its own race. The persistent drunkard is lower down in the scale of creation than Darwin's ape at the beginning.

On the same ruinous scale, the sluggard wastes his life. He sleeps all thrift out of his shop; sleeps all friends out of his company; sleeps all grace out of his heart; sleeps all religion, and order, and prosperity out of his home; sleeps all conscience out of his dealings; sleeps himself into nothing and into hell. The world has a multitude of these triflers in luxurious laziness, worthless to community, mopes and encumbrances in society, sinking, for lack of employment, into shame, and poverty, and death. God pity the poor fool who despises work, who lives to feed and to sleep! He is not quite so dangerous, perhaps, as the drunkard, but he is more degraded and more repulsive. Christianity proposes to give men and women every-day work; and unless it ungloves the hand and prompts the foot on errands of duty, it fails of its mission upon the earth.

THE GRADED ALPHABET.

A is the young man's first glass of ale,
B is the beer which next will prevail,
C is the cider, so simple at first,
Causing in future unquenchable thirst,
D is the dram taken morn, noon, or eve,
E is the extra one—at eleven, I believe—
F is the flip thought so good for a cold,
G is the gin not so pure as of old,
H is the hotel, where often he goes,
I is the inner room he so well knows,
J is the jug he there fills to the brim,
K is the knocking of conscience within,
L is the landlord, who smiles as you drink,
M is your money he's getting, I think,
N is the nightmare which visits your brain,
O is the orgies of a midnight train,
P is the poor, penniless pauper you become,
Q is the quarrel, the product of rum,
R is the ruin rum brings to your door,
S is the suffering ne'er known before,
T is the tremens, and mark this as true:
They make few calls ere death must ensue
U is the undertaker who comes to your aid,
V is the valley where your body is laid,
W is the wretchedness, wailing, and woe
'X ecrable drunkards alone can know,
Y is the yearning for misspent time,
Z is the zenith of the drunkard's clime.

DRUNK IN THE STREET.

DRUNK in the street!
A woman arrested to-day in the city!
Comely and young, the paper said;
Scarcely twenty, the item read;
A woman and wife—kind angels pity!
Drunk in the street!

Drunk in the street!
Yes, crazy with liquor; her brain on fire!
Reeling, plunging, stagg'ring along,
Singing a strain of a childish song;
At last she stumbles and falls in the mire—
Drunk in the street!

Drunk in the street!
What news to send the dear ones home,
Who're wond'ring what has detained so long
The wife and mother, yet think no wrong!
The day is waning, the night is come—
Drunk in the street!

Drunk in the street!
Drag her away to a station-bed;
Helpless, senseless, take her away;
Shut her up from the light of day;
Would, for the sake of her friends, she were dead!
Drunk in the street!

Draw nigh and look!
On a couch of straw in a station-cell
Is lying a form of matchless mould,
With hair dishevelled, so pale and cold,
Yet tainting the air with the fumes of hell!
Draw nigh and look!

How sad the sight!
The sunlight is streaming across the floor,
It rouses the sleeper to life again;
But, oh! the anguish, the grief, the pain,
As thoughts of her shame come crowding o'er—
How sad the sight!

But hark! a sound!
The bolt flies back, she is told to rise;
Her friends are waiting to take her home.
They know it all, yet in love they come;
But with speechless lips and tearless eyes—
The lost one's found.

Behold her now!
She goes all trembling with shame away,
Her brain still clouded with fumes of rum,
And turns her tottering feet towards home
And the hearts she left but yesterday—
How diff'rent now!

Close we the scene!
Fall, O night! o'er the saddest sight
That ever appeared to mortal view;
Shield, O skies! with your vaulted blue
Shut, O gates of memory! tight—
Close we the scene!

E. B. WICKS, M.D.

A WORD TO YOUNG MEN.

How many of our most promising young men does intemperance ensnare, and, by its impetuous torrent, sweep away to infamy and the grave! Many young men have yielded to the solicitations of their associates and taken a glass who never intended to take another, or at least not to make a practice of it; but when they have once tasted the cup, they ventured again and again; and thus led on step by step, they soon become drunkards. The vice of intemperance hurries its victim with the violence of passion, captivates him by the allurements of pleasure; he yields to the impulse, merely because he cannot resist it; reason remonstrates, conscience endeavors to check him, but all in vain. Having once allowed the strong passion to gain the ascendant, he has thrown himself in the middle of a torrent, against which he may sometimes faintly struggle, but the impetuosity of the stream bears him along. In this situation he is so far from being free that he is not master of himself; he does not go, but is driven, tossed, and impelled, passive like a ship to the violence of the waves.

How often have unworthy friendships, imprudent and vicious associates, engaged young men, unwarily at first, and at length habitually in a fatal course of folly and crime! Let me ask where has the dissolute young man contracted these vices, which, in spite of his convictions, are dragging him captive at their will; where the worthless gambler learned his infamous trade; where the contemptible lounger acquired his habits of idleness; where the prodigal, the intemperate, the profligate, where have they corrupted all their powers, both of body and of soul? Was it not in vicious society, whose pleasure is in the intoxicating bowl? Pause, young man, and fly from the haunts of "club-rooms," saloons, and tippling-shops, where intoxicating liquors are sold. Perhaps you may feel unconcerned on this subject, because you never were drunkards. But let me tell you all drunkards felt just so before they were enslaved and brutalized by intemperance. What young man can look upon the dreadful picture I have but imperfectly drawn, and not perceive his danger? A mournful cry comes from the prison-cell, and cautions all to flee from the accursed enemy of our peace and liberty. The grave, too, into which so many have gone down, the unhappy victims of inebriation, speaks in solemn tones to escape from the unrelenting enemy. A voice also, as within, the unerring monitor, warns all to beware of the insidious foe. All, all speak in a voice like the rushing of mighty waters against intemperance.

Young men, I pray you heed this advice, and avoid the dens of darkness and destruction; go not near the sinks of iniquity; pass by them as you would a pestilence which is sure death. Your good example will do much, very much, towards checking the progress of the abominable practice of rum-drinking. Abstain from the practice yourself, and do all you can to save those of your age from falling into the vice of intemperance, which is making so many pests of society and cumberers of the earth; which is robbing them of their characters, blunting their minds, hardening their hearts, and searing their consciences. If you desire to be respected, abstain from the appearance of evil, lest you be drawn into temptation. Resist—ay, that is the word—resist, with all the energy you possess, the beginning, and shun the occasions of so dangerous a vice as that of intemperance.

A. L.

The Mouse and Her Promise.

A little mouse fell into a brewery-vat,
And lay in distress till espied by a cat;
"O pussy! kind pussy! do help me, I pray!"
"If I do," said the cat, "you will run right away."
"Oh! no, Mrs. Puss, I will certainly stay."
So in went a paw—a struggle and splash,
And Mousy was safe, and off like a flash.
"Contemptible wretch! without honor or shame,
Is it thus," cried the cat, "that you perjure your name?"

"Hold! hold! Mrs. Puss, I will show in a trice
That my sense of honor is exceedingly nice;
But who could expect me," said mouse, with a snicker,
"A promise to keep that I made when in liquor?"

Make it a Political Question.

We must take the subject out of the domain of social and religious questions, and insist on making it a political one. Everything that appertains to the common weal is a fair subject of legislation. The science of politics deals with the commonwealth. And is not the mainspring of almost all the pauperism and most of the crime committed in the land a suitable topic for political discussion? Yes; but we are met with the cry, The "freedom of the subject" must not be endangered. There is a limit to the interference of law. Individual liberty must not be sacrificed. Well, I grant that government ought not to interfere in anything which concerns the life of an individual, unless the interests of others are affected by that life. And are not the interests of others affected by the life of a drunkard? Is his example nothing? The pauperization of his family nothing? The brutal treatment of his children nothing? The diminution of productive labor in consequence of this vice nothing? The perpetuation of this evil—God visiting the sins of the father upon the children to the third and fourth generation—is this nothing? Are not the interests of society affected by a vice which fills jails, starves families, shatters reason, and creates murderers? Is the depopulation of our country not a sufficiently important matter to occupy the attention of government? I sha'n't attempt statistical proof—all can do it for themselves; I should thank God if I be mistaken, but I believe that the number of men who are killed prematurely by drink is simply frightful. Legislatures give good heed to everything that will increase our population, and we are all deeply interested in inducing immigration to develop our resources as a nation. But if we could only, by sanitary arrangements, save the lives of the children born in the land, and by a prohibitory law save the thousands of young men who die annually of intemperance, we should not be so dependent on foreign emigration as we now are. And let it be remembered that it is not the refuse of the population, the offscouring of humanity, who are alone the victims of this plague. No; it fastens on the finest intellects. It selects for its prey the most highly cultivated minds, and drags into degradation and death men whose genius might have enriched the world. Again, I ask, what is self-government worth if it is afraid to touch the root and cause of such a national disaster? Sure I am that if all the deaths from intemperance every year, instead of being diffused over the large area of the country, were concentrated in a smaller area, say the distilleries, six months would not elapse before the general conscience of the people would clamor for a remedy; they would be thunderstruck at the loss incurred, and would force upon their representatives the conviction that modes of generating wealth so destructive of human life demand immediate prohibition.

ONWARD AND UPWARD.

THE ancient days of chivalry are past,
  So long renowned in song and story,
Their glories chanted and their praises sung
  By many a wandering bard and poet hoary,
Whose wild and ever-changing measure told
  Of quivering lance and prancing steed,
Of knightly combat and of gleaming mail,
  Of gorgeous pageantry and valorous deed.

And listening to his story in the hush
  Of eve, how many an aged pulse beat high,
And youthful cheeks were tinged with hope's fair flush,
  As youthful hearts resolved to "Do or die!"
And they who conquered, what was their reward?
  Was it for sparkling gems or gold
They perilled life, and both the young and brave
  Were lying 'neath the willow, motionless and cold?

'Twas for a name, an empty song of praise,
  A laurel wreath that faded ere the sun
Came o'er the hills, and gilded with his rays
  The scene—now still—where victory was won.
But now we sing a higher, nobler theme
  Than tales of chivalry in by-gone days;
For this shall minstrels strike their richest chords,
  And poets breathe their softest, sweetest lays.

The strife is on the temperance battle-field;
  There right shall be the bloodless sword,
Truth an impenetrable shield,
  And for a motto, "Onward" is the word.
"Onward and Upward" let the echoes ring
  O'er valley green or barren hill.
Through crowded cities, with their dust and din,
  "Onward and Upward" is the watchword still,
Till Drink, the tyrant, from his throne be hurled,
And white-robed Temperance rule o'er all the world.

A Righteous Demand.

I know I am right when I say that the traffic in intoxicating liquors is at war with every interest of society, is in deadly hostility to every man, woman, and child to all eternity, and that such business ought not to be permitted to be carried on in a civilized and Christian community. I know it ought to be prohibited; I am sure that the people will come to it, and that the country will be ready for it by-and-by. The grog-shops, as they exist in this country, are the cause of greater evils than all other causes of evil combined. No man can deny that it is so. We demand that they shall be abolished by law. I submit, if any man objects to our proposition, he is bound to show that more good comes from the grog-shops than evil. The law-making power comes and shuts up the gambling-saloon, the lottery-shop, and the house of ill-fame, because they are inconsistent with the general good. There is the grog-shop; shut it up. It is ten thousand times more injurious than all other things combined. Railways kill a great many people, and by better precautionary measures life would be safer on railroads than it now is; but is there any proposition to abolish railroads? No; because more good than evil comes from the railway. Steamboats produce immense mischief by explosions and collisions; but it is not proposed to abolish steam navigation, because more good than evil comes from the use of steamboats. I defy any man to show that good comes from the grog-shops, to the amount of a single farthing, to the nation or to the people, while the evils flowing from them are greater than all other existing evils in society. No man can deny that the traffic in intoxicating drinks is an infinite mischief to the nation, and brings misery to the people, and that the entire suppression of that traffic would be an infinite advantage to the nation and an incalculable blessing to the people. If he is a distiller and a member of the whiskey-ring, he cannot deny that.

Who objects? The people who are making fortunes out of it and the moderate drinkers. And this is their position: they must acknowledge that the liquor traffic effects the mischief which I have represented, and its abolition will be a great benefit to society; but they say: "We will not submit to it, because it would put us to inconvenience to get our drink." Independent of the question of pecuniary interest, any man who objects to this movement, it is upon that ground, and upon no other.

NEAL DOW.

THE MODERN CAIN.

"AM I my brother's keeper?"
Long ago,
When first the human heart-strings felt the touch
Of death's cold fingers; when upon the earth,
Shroudless and coffinless, death's first-born lay,
Slain by the hand of violence, the wail of human grief arose:
"My son, my son!
Awake thee from this strange and awful sleep;
A mother mourns thee, and her tears of grief
Are falling on thy pale, unconscious brow:
Awake, and bless her with thy wonted smile."

In vain, in vain! That sleeper never woke;
His murderer fled, but on his brow was fixed
A stain which baffled wear and washing. As he fled,
A voice pursued him to the wilderness:
"Where is thy brother, Cain?"

"Am I my brother's keeper?"
Cain, Cain,
Thou art thy brother's keeper, and his blood
Cries up to heaven against thee! Every stone
Will find a tongue to curse thee, and the winds
Will ever wail this question in thy ear:
"Where is thy brother?" Every sight and sound
Will mind thee of the lost.

I saw a man
Deal death unto his brother. Drop by drop
The poison was distilled for cursèd gold;
And in the wine-cup's ruddy glow sat death,
Invisible to that poor trembling slave.
He seized the cup, he drank the poison down,
Rushed forth into the streets—home had he none—
Staggered and fell, and miserably died!
They buried him—ah! little recks it where
His bloated form was given to the worms.

Once had he friends;
A happy home was his, and love was his.
His Mary loved him, and around him played
His smiling children. Oh! a dream of joy
Were those unclouded years; and, more than all,
He had an interest in the world above.
The big "Old Bible" lay upon the stand,
And he was wont to read its sacred page,
And then to pray: "Our Father, bless the poor,
And save the tempted from the tempter's art;
Save us from sin, and ever let us be
United in thy love; and may we meet,
When life's last scenes are o'er, around the throne."
Thus prayed he—thus lived he. Years passed,
And o'er the sunshine of that happy home
A cloud came from the pit; the fatal bolt
Fell from that cloud. The towering tree
Was shivered by the lightning's vengeful stroke,
And laid its coronal of glory low.
A happy home was ruined; want and woe
Played with his children, and the joy of youth
Left their sweet faces, no more to return.
His Mary's face grew pale and paler still,
Her eyes were dimmed with weeping, and her soul
Went out through those blue portals. Mary died.
And yet he wept not. At the demon's call,

He drowned his sorrow in the maddening bowl;
And when they buried her from sight, he sank
In drunken stupor by her new-made grave!
His friend was gone—he never had another—
And the world shrank from him; all save one,
And *he* still plied the bowl with deadly drug,
And bade him drink, forget his God, and die!

He died!
Cain! Cain! where is thy brother now?
Lives he still—if dead, still where is he?
Where? In heaven? Go read the sacred page.
"No drunkard shall inherit there."
Who sent him to the pit? Who dragged him down?
Who bound him hand and foot? Who smiled and smiled
While yet the hellish work went on? Who grasped
His gold, his health, his life, his hope, his all?
Who saw his Mary fade and die? Who saw
His beggared children wandering in the streets?
Speak, coward! If thou hast a tongue,
Tell why with hellish art you slew A MAN.

"Where is my brother?"
"Am I my brother's keeper?"
Ah! man, a deeper mark is on your brow
Than that of Cain. Accursèd was the name
Of him who slew a righteous man, whose soul
Was ripe for heaven; thrice accursèd he
Whose art malignant sinks a soul to hell.

PROF. E. EVANS EDWARDS.

Work and Results.

A GENTLEMAN said to me the other day: "The temperance cause is dead." It is not dead, for it was born in the church of Christ, and that which is born there can never die. Right is to triumph in the end. You and I will not live to see it, but it will come. Nero sat on the throne, clothed in purple, and at his nod men trembled. In the Mamertine dungeon a man was writing a letter to Timothy to send him his cloak, for he was shivering in one of the dungeons of the Roman capital. Years rolled on, and right and wrong contended with each other. The former died a miserable suicide, but the prisoner wrote on and finished his letter: "I have fought a good fight, I have finished my course, I have kept the faith"—words which have comforted millions for generations. And the world could better afford to lose all the words of eloquence that ever fell from the lips of Roman orators, than to lose one word of what the chained prisoner wrote in his dungeon. My experience has led me to this conclusion, that we trust too much even to our organizations and to our efforts. We are in too much of a hurry; we want results immediately. We do a thing and want results to come at once, forgetting that with the Lord one day is as a thousand years, and a thousand years as one day. It is God's work, and not ours—we are workers. If a man stands as a machine, and if he is connected by a band of living faith with God Almighty, he is doing his work as he will, where he will, and when he will, and occupies the highest position a man can occupy in this world. God is the motive power, and our work is simply nothing in comparison with him. Then as we put forth our efforts, let us make our appeal to him.

I remember (and I do not know whether it was a legend or not) that a missionary party were passing over the prairie, when one of them exclaimed, "See, see that red glare; what is it?" They looked and watched, and one old trapper, shading his eye with his hand, cried out, "The prairie is on fire, and it is spreading at the rate of twenty miles an hour. It will destroy us, and nothing will be left but a few charred bones to tell of the party passing over the prairie." "What shall be done?" The trapper cried, "We must fight fire with fire. Work! work! Pull up the grass; make the circle larger, larger. larger! Quick, quick, I feel the heat upon my brow! Quick for your lives! pull up the grass! pull up the grass! Now for the matches!"

They searched, and found two. Hastily they struck one, and it failed—utterly failed. One match! and the fire coming in the distance, leaping with its forked tongues through the dry grass, at twenty miles an hour! Only one match! The missionary, baring his brow, said, "God help us; for thy great name's sake, help us in our extremity." Every heart prompted the words, and the lips uttered "Amen." They struck the match; it caught fire, and the grass was ignited; and as the fire swept round them in a circle, they marched on triumphant, exultant, victorious.

Our instrumentalities—Temperance Societies, Bands of Hope, Sons of Temperance, Good Templars, whatever they may be—are as feeble as that one match. Before we put forth our efforts, then, let us reverently ask God to help us for his great name's sake; and we, with those we have worked for, shall stand in the circle unharmed while the flames play away at the distance—and we stand saved, not by our own efforts alone, but by our own efforts blessed and acknowledged by him in whose hands are the destinies of all men.

John B. Gough.

DIALOGUES.

DIALOGUES.

BAD COMPANY.

CHARACTERS.—*Dora, George Moore, Carrie, Mat, and Policeman.*

(*George with cigar-stump in his fingers, as though he had been smoking. Enter Dora and Carrie.*)

DORA. George Moore, you're a mean boy, if you *are* my cousin. How dare you tear my TEMPERANCE BANNER to light your old cigar? (*Holds up half of a paper.*)

GEORGE. I'm sure I didn't suppose it was of any use here; nobody needs it in this house, for there are no whiskey-topers about.

CARRIE. There is a *tobacco*-toper about, and that's bad enough, Phew! what a horrid smell! I do think, Mr. George Moore, that if you are so depraved as to find it absolutely necessary to smoke, you ought to go out into the woods, where the birds and beasts have room enough to get out of your way; for I must say it is outrageous for you or any other person to poison the air that others have to breathe.

G. Really, Carrie, you are very personal. I deny your assertion that I find it "absolutely necessary to smoke"; for I can stop now, and never smoke another cigar. But I think smoking and drinking wine are harmless indulgences.

D. Harmless indulgences, indeed! If they are, why do they lead so many men and boys into other and worse habits that end in the station-house or prison? If you want us to believe that you *can* give up cigars and wine, *prove it* by joining our Band of Hope at its next meeting, and give up Mat Brown's society.

G. I'm sure I'm no worse for associating with him; and as for joining the Band, he would never get done poking fun at me if I should.

C. A person who is ashamed to do right for fear of being laughed at is very weak indeed; and I insist that you *have* learned evil ways from Mat Brown, for you never smoked or drank wine till you became intimate with him.

(*A peculiar whistle is heard at the door.*)

G. There's Mat now, whistling for me! I'll run out and see him. (*Goes out.*)

D. The page of my BANNER is torn that has Aunt Julia's "Temperance Catechism" on it, and I have not read it yet. It vexes me to think an old cigar was lighted with it.

C. If George don't give up his bad habits and keep better company, we'll cut his acquaintance.

(*Enter George and Mat hastily.*)

G. (*excited.*) I say, girls, can't you hide Mat somewhere? A policeman's after him, and—

(*Enter Policeman.*)

POLICEMAN. I guess the young ladies won't trouble themselves about the thieving scamp. (*Takes Mat by the shoulder.*) I advise this other young fellow to keep better company, or *he* will be my next prisoner.

G. What has he done, sir? Haven't you made a mistake?

MAT (*defiantly*). Yes, he's made a big mistake; and if he don't let me go, my father will make him pay for it. (*While speaking, puts his hand suddenly and slyly into George's jacket-pocket. Policeman seizes his hand and holds it up, with a watch in it.*)

P. Of course I've made an *awful* big mistake. He didn't steal this watch from the jeweller's—of course not; and he didn't try to slip it in your pocket to make you appear the thief—oh! no. Come along, my honest youth; I'll risk the mistake. (*Pulls him along through the doorway, resisting and muttering.*) Come along, and try how you like the lock-up.

G. Well, well, who would have believed it? And I thought he was such a nice fellow! Carrie, you can propose my name to the Band of Hope. Dora, I'll subscribe for THE YOUTH'S TEMPERANCE BANNER, and beware of bad company hereafter.

MRS. NELLIE H. BRADLEY.

NEW CIDER.

CHARACTERS.—*James and Dwight.*

JAMES. Good-evening, Cousin Dwight. Glad to see you. Come, go around to our house; got something particularly nice for you.

DWIGHT. Good! What is it?

J. Some new cider. Uncle Harper was in town yesterday, and brought us half a barrel, and it's real nice. Mother said you ought to have some, as you are so particular what you drink, and that I must ask you to come around for a drink.

D. Much obliged, but I suppose you know that I do not drink cider?

J. You don't, eh? Why, I'm sure that I've seen you.

D. Where?

J. Why—why, let me see. Why, when we were out at grandma's one Thanksgiving. Don't you remember?

D. Oh! yes; a year ago or more. That was before I found out so much about cider as I know now.

J. Found out about cider! That's all humbug. Found out it was in the pledge, I suppose.

D. I'm pledged against it; that is reason enough why I should not take it. But there are very good reasons for pledging against it, I can tell you.

J. Well, now, what are the reasons for a boy's not drinking cider? It is nothing but apple-juice, and can't do anybody any harm if he should drink a gallon of it.

D. But I've seen farmers get boozy on it. Grandma's hired man did when we were there. And I knew a carpenter once get crazy drunk on it, and chase another man all over the building with an adze; and he meant to hurt him, too, and he would if he had not fallen and hurt himself.

J. Some quarrelsome fellow, no doubt, that just wanted an excuse for a fight.

D. On the contrary, he was very peaceable when not poisoned out of his senses with alcohol; and they say cider is one of the worst things to get drunk on.

J. How can it be? What is it but just apple-juice, anyway?

D. It is apple-juice rotted, that is what it is.

J. Rotted! How do you make that out?

D. Why, you mash up an apple, and let it stand, and how long before it would rot? Well, the juice rots just as quick, and sometimes quicker, and then it turns into something else—alcohol and carbonic acid—and it is no more fit to drink than the rotten apples are fit to eat. Let it stand a while longer, and it will turn into vinegar.

J. Well, this is not so bad.

D. No, not so bad as the alcohol; but you would not think of asking me to drink a glass of it because it is "only just apple-juice"?

J. Oh! well, I am not talking about vinegar nor rotten apple-juice. This new cider that uncle brought us is not rotten at all.

D. *New* cider, is it? That is, it was new the day it was made, and so of course it was new the next day, for it could not grow old in one day. When does it get to be old?

J. I suppose this is just made, or they wouldn't call it new.

D. Cider is made in the fall when the apples are gathered, usually in October. So this must be three or four months old. [Let the time be fixed according to the date when the dialogue is used.] There has been time enough for it to rot a good deal. I have very little doubt there is alcohol enough in it to go to the head pretty quickly.

J. It did go to my head last night, and I thought that was the best part of it. It makes a fellow feel real funny.

D. Funny? It makes him act like a fool, and feel like one too, if he only knew enough to judge of his own feelings. That's the way it generally serves those who get drunk.

J. Get drunk! You don't mean to say that I got drunk?

D. It seems you did, according to your own account, whether I say it or not. What is getting drunk but being poisoned by alcohol—having it go to the head, and affect the brain?

J. Oh! well, it didn't affect me much, only a little.

D. Then I suppose you were drunk only a little, but just as surely drunk as though it was done with whiskey. The alcohol in the cider is the same as that in the whiskey, and many a drunkard has begun on cider when a boy. You would better look out for yourself.

J. All that fuss about a little apple-juice!

D. I'm not so bewitched after apple-juice that I'll travel that road after it, and take it after it is rotten. Please make my compliments to Aunt Kate, and tell her that, when I am thirsty, I have plenty of things to drink that are better and safer than rotten apple-juice.

AUNT JULIA.

DIALOGUE ON SMOKING.

CHARACTERS.—*Willie and Frank.*

WILLIE. See here, Frank, I hear a bad report about you.

FRANK. About me! Why, what have I been doing?

W. I hear you have been smoking.

F. That's a false report; but I can tell you who has.

W. Well, I am glad you have not, and I hope none of our temperance band have.

F. Yes. I saw Dan Simpleton strutting about the other day, puffing a cigar, and trying to swell up to man-like dimensions.

W. He ought to be ashamed. What does he do it for?

F. Oh! because he sees *men* do it, I suppose.

W. Yes; but men drink rum, and swear, and do other bad things.

F. Well, he sees other boys do it, and a good many of them too.

W. Does he see any boys smoke who do not swear, strut about on Sunday, and do other like things too?

F. That's a hard question; but he thinks it makes him look big, and what's the harm in trying to get big?

W. No harm, perhaps, but I guess a cigar don't help much. I think it rather shows an empty garret, or one in which there is not much but smoke.

F. Well, Dan did say it made him light-headed and everything look green.

W. You know green glasses make things look that way, but the green is in the glasses.

F. Yes, and I suppose the green was in Dan's head, too.

W. And you may set it down as a rule that the head of a boy who puffs cigars don't need to be made any lighter or greener either.

HIS WORST ENEMY.

CHARACTERS.—*Walter and Charles.*

WALTER. Did you hear that terrible racket last night, Charley?

CHARLES. No; takes a good deal to wake me up. What was the matter?

W. Why, Captain George had one of his worst times—regular crazy drunk; you can't think how he went on.

C. What did he do?

W. Enough, I should think, to make him ashamed to show himself among decent folks.

C. Did you get scared any?

W. Some. You see it was along after midnight, when I woke all of a sudden. I thought first there must be a fire; then I heard some one hollering. I jumped up, and, looking out of the window, I could just see a man on horseback riding down the stone sidewalk. Hearing some one down-stairs, I went down and found father, who had been waked by the noise. He said it was Captain George.

C. What was he yelling about?

W. Oh! he didn't know what he was doing—all out of his head. He seemed to think he was down South fighting the rebs. He was ordering his men into position, and driving about terribly excited, as if he was right in a battle. I felt sorry for the poor old horse, for he whacked him about cruelly.

C. Did any one try to stop him?

W. Yes, father and two or three of the neighbors after a while got him off the horse, and took him home.

C. Captain George always seems such a kind, pleasant man when he is sober, but he acts so that no one cares anything for him. Strange that he will drink so!

W. If he had signed the pledge, as we boys have, and always kept it, he might have been one of the first men in town.

C. He don't look or act worth much now. Every one says he is fast digging for himself a drunkard's grave.

W. What I saw last night and heard this morning, Charlie, has made me hate rum worse than ever before. I am going to love our Temperance Society, and work harder for it than I have done.

C. You told me what you saw last night; what was it you heard this morning that has made you so excited on the temperance question?

W. When I came to breakfast, I saw that mother had been crying, and was very quiet and sad. After prayers, we sat down by the window talking over Captain George's strange actions. Then she told me all about him—what a beautiful boy he was, how every one loved and petted him; then he went away to school, bad associates led him into bad habits, smoking and drinking just a little. When he came home, folks saw he was changed. When the war broke out, he went into the army, fought well for his country, but he let his worst enemy—rum—conquer him.

C. What a sad story! I am glad that we can associate with temperance boys and girls. We must work to get all we can in with us.

W. Yes, for one thing is certain—if we never touch anything that intoxicates, we shall not be drunkards, going about the streets despised by all, without mind, influence, or character.

C. Yes, as our teacher says, we want to get in the way that leads to the springs of living waters, then we shall keep far away from the path that goes down to the drunkard's grave.

E. B. S.

THE FOUNTAIN AND THE STILL.

CHARACTERS.—*Fountain, Still and Drunkard.*

FOUNTAIN. I am the Fountain. STILL. I'm the Still.
F. My mission's for good. S. And mine's not ill.
F. I sparkle in gems of morning dew.
S. And I in the wine-cup's ruddy hue.
F. I cool the poor man's heated brow,
When from his daily toil returning.
S. I drown his cares in the rich, red flow
Of the ruby wine. F. 'Tis the cup of burning.
I'm queen of the mountain-brooks!
S. And I
Rule o'er the streams that dash foaming by
From yon distillery's heart of fire.
Onward they flow, and never tire;
Leaping on high, their spray they fling,
And they laugh as they come, and merrily sing.
F. My throne is the top of yon mountain high,
And those gorgeous clouds my canopy;
My sceptre, the rainbow; my crown, the spray;
Its pearls are the dewdrops; the first bright ray
Of the morning sun, as he wheels his car
Upward through the ethereal blue,
Decks me with gems more beautiful far
Than all the splendor that earth e'er knew.
S. In yon gilded palace I hold my court,
Where the song and jest go merrily round;
Where the wine-cup sparkles, and mirth and sport
Hold sway till the midnight air resounds.
My wand of power is a goblet bright,
And all bow before its magic might;
A vine-leaf wreath on my brow I bear,
And its purple clusters for gems I wear.

F. Dashing down the hillside,
Rippling through the meadows,
Gliding through the forests
In sunshine and in shadows;
Ever moving onward
With its mellow laughter,
Sparkling, foaming, gushing,
Comes the crystal water.

S. Full of life and beauty,
Blushing the rose's hue,
Chasing the cares of the weary
With its cup of heavenly dew;
Changing sorrow to gladness,
Bringing joy divine,
Giver of bliss immortal,
Glitters the ruddy wine.

F. Deep within the bosom of the earth,
Hidden far from mortal sight,
In a fairy grotto I had my birth.
Drop by drop, like diamonds bright,
Fell the dewy gems; the light
From a hundred fairy lamps shone round.
Each lamp was a jewel; in silence profound
They waited the hour when, freed from the thrall
Of my elfin prison-house, merry and clear,
I sprang forth into light on the mountain tall,
Where to earthly ken I first appear
In a mimic torrent adown the steep.
O'er my rocky bed my course I keep;
A rippling brook down the mountain-side,
A gliding stream through the meadows wide,
A mighty river, hastening on,
Till at ocean's bounds the goal is won.

S. From the time when our second father rode
On the heaving bosom of the flood,
My life-giving cup has banished care,
With its sparkling nectar, rich and rare.

The golden beams of the sun so bright
Deck in beauty the wine.
[*Enter a drunkard.*]
DRUNK. (hic) It made me tight.

F. Behold yon wretched man! With faltering tread
He staggers on his way; trembling and slow
He walks; his blinded eyes and aching head
Refuse to point the path. DRUNK. (hic) I guess that's so.

S. 'Tis not my fault if some weak brains
Yield to the power that lies within the bowl,
And quaff too deep its contents, till the soul
Awhile forgets its earthly cares and pains—

D. And gets (hic) most gloriously drunk, (hic) and when
He tries to (hic) walk, the path an't wide enough, and then
The ground comes up to meet him, and he goes
To meet (hic) the ground; falls down, and (hic) barks his nose.

F. Poor victim of the tempter's fatal power!
Break off thy chains; no longer shrink and cower
Beneath that tyrant's fascinating eye.
Here, sign the pledge, and in temptation's hour
'Twill give you strength to make the monster fly.

S. I love not scenes of misery and woe;
My office 'tis to comfort man, not pain;
And if by chance unhappiness should strew
The drunkard's path, sure I'm not to blame.
But since my presence is unwelcome here,
I'll go; some more congenial sphere
I'll find, where joy and happiness abound. [*Exit.*

D. And (hic) where poor drunken fools like me (hic) an't found.

F. Oh! will you heed my warning voice, and break the fatal spell?
Say, will you sign this talisman? The songs of joy will swell

From angel tongues in concord sweet around the throne above.
It matters not how fallen you are; remember "God is love."
Brother— DRUNK. What! call me brother! Speak not that hallowed name
To one so base, so low, deep sunk in sin and shame.
'Tis the first word of kindness I've heard this many a year.
It brings to memory one that's gone—a much-loved sister dear.
Oh! I remember well, too well, the evening that she died.
The sun was setting in the west; she called me to her side,
And made me promise on my knees, before her spirit fled,
That I would meet her there, in heaven above; she said
She saw the angels waiting to carry her away,
And with a smile upon her lip, she left her house of clay,
To join her waiting friends in that bright world of love,
Where pain and sorrow are no more; and left me here to rove,
Friendless and homeless, through the dreary earth.
The tempter found me, and I fell an easy prey.
I drank to drown my sorrow; swiftly I trod the way
That leads to the drunkard's grave. Oh! can I ever know
Again the joy that once I knew? And is there here below
Hope for the fallen one, who, lost in sin and dark despair,

Is rushing onward to his doom without a thought
or care?

F. Yes, yes, there's mercy still for you; break from
your fetters! Lo,
The angels wait in silence, turning here below
Their anxious looks; from the high battlements
of heaven
They watch the scene. Oh! may a life long given
To wickedness be blest by such a close
As may atone for guilt that's past and bring a
blest repose.

D. Give me the paper; let me sign the pledge. [*Signs
his name.*] And now
Heaven grant me aid, God give me strength, to
keep this solemn vow.

BOTH. And may our heavenly Parent grant his blessing on this hour,
When an immortal soul is saved from out the
tempter's power.

GEORGE C. CRANE, *in Zion's Herald.*

WHAT RUM WILL DO.

FOR FIVE CHARACTERS.

First Voice.

RUM will scorch and sear the brain,
Rum will mad the heart with pain,
Rum will bloat the flesh with fire,
And eternal thirst inspire.

Second Voice.

Rum will clothe with rags your back,
Make you walk a crooked track,
Change your meat to naked bones,
And to wrath your gentle tones.

Third Voice.

Rum will rob the head of sense,
Rum will rob the purse of pence,
Rum will rob the mouth of food,
And the soul of heavenly good.

Fourth Voice.

Rum the jails with men will fill,
And the dungeon's gloomy cell;
It rouses passion's deadly hate,
And pours its curses o'er the state.

Fifth Voice.

Rum the Christian's love will cool,
Make him break the golden rule,
Bind his soul to error's bands,
And to evil turn his hands.

All Together in Concert.

This maddening drink we will not take,
Our solemn pledge we will not break;
O Father! keep us by thy hand,
And guard from sin this youthful band.

BE KIND TO THE DRUNKARD.

CHARACTERS.— *Matthew and Stephen.*

(*Matthew reading.*)

STEPHEN (*enters whistling*). O you old book-worm! you've lost some jolly fun by not going out with us boys.

MAT. (*looking up*). What kind of fun?

S. Well, I don't mind telling you, if you'll ask me to take a seat.

M. (*rising and placing a chair*). Do be seated, Mr. Clayton.

S. (*seating himself*). We found a chap lying out by the school-fence as drunk as a dog—

M. Stop a bit! Did you ever see a dog drunk?

S. Of course not; but you know very well what I mean.

M. I suppose you wish to convey the impression that he was very drunk?

S. Yes. You are *so* fussy, Mat. Well, we tickled his ears with straws, and he rolled over and grunted like a hog; then we put his hat on inside out, and pulled his hair through the holes in the crown; then we blacked his nose with burnt cork, and painted his cheeks yellow and his chin blue. Oh! he was the most comical picture you ever saw; I burst two buttons off my vest laughing at him.

M. Stephen, I'm ashamed of you! You'll keep the company of those good-for-nothing boys until you will get into serious trouble.

S. Why, what harm did we do? We only teased him without hurting him.

M. It is wrong to torment or ridicule any one who is unfortunate; and I hope you will never do it again. But where is the poor fellow now?

S. I did not finish. We got an old piece of matting, and were trying to roll him up in it, when he scrambled on to his feet and swore till the air was blue, and then tumbled over again. Just then a man suddenly came round the corner, and threatened to cane us if we did not leave; and he would have done it, too, for his cane was big and his arm was strong.

M. I wish he *had* caned you all soundly. What happened next?

S. I don't like to tell you, Mat; but you'll be sure to hear of it, so I might as well out with it. You see that (*takes handkerchief from his pocket and holds it up, all streaked and spotted with black and yellow*). Well, as I started to run with the rest, he caught me, pulled me along to the hydrant, and made me get this wet and wash the drunken fellow's face. I tell you, I was mad enough to bite them both.

M. Served you just right. I guess that was more than you bargained for. What next?

S. The cold water sobered the man some; for he got up, and I took my leave. But I've got news for you. Mamma received a letter informing us that Uncle Stephen Parker had returned from Europe, and was coming to stay at our house for a month; everything has been turned topsy-turvy, and lots of new things bought.

M. Why do they make so much extra preparation for a man they have never seen?

S. Don't you know? He is your uncle as well as mine; but I was named for him, and, though he has never seen me, he has said that he intends to do something handsome for me; he is very rich, and has no family. Mamma gave me a good lecture this morning in regard to my behavior; for he is very queer about some things.

M. And so Uncle Parker is coming at last! How I do wish we were not so poor; for I know mother would like to have him stay with us. But if he is rich, he has been used to much better than we can afford; and your folks are fixed so nicely he will be very comfortable there.

S. Of course he will! And now I must run home, and see if everything is ready. Good-by. (*Runs out.*)

M. (*walking slowly back and forth*). This is news indeed! It does seem as though *we* ought to have whatever Uncle Parker can spare; for we have a hard struggle to get along since father died. But I suppose it is all right. I am thankful mother has the promise of better pay for her sewing; she ought to get as much again. I expect that last job is ready for me to take home. (*Goes out.*)

Scene II.

(*Mat. and Stephen enter from opposite sides, if possible.*)

M. (*joyfully*). I've seen Uncle Parker, Stephen!

S. (*angrily*). And so have I; but tell me quickly how *you* happened to walk *into* his good graces just as *I* walked *out*.

M. All I know about it is just this: After you left yesterday, I started to carry home mother's sewing, and I came across a drunken man, who, I suppose, was the one you were telling about. As he staggered across a gutter, he fell and cut his head. I felt sorry for him, and washed off the blood, and tried to help him up; but I was giving it up, when some one behind me said, "Who is that you are trying to help?" And turning, I saw the man with the cane. I told him I did not know, and he helped the man to get up; and then his wife, who had been looking for him, came and led him away. The man with the cane then asked me my name, and, when I told him, he exclaimed, "My dear boy, I am your Uncle Parker!" He then went home with me, and talked a long time with mother, after which he went to your house.

S. Yes, he walked in unexpectedly; and, after a talk with mother and sister, enquired for me. I heard mother call, and rushed in like a steam-engine, not knowing who was there. But I stopped suddenly; for there was the man with the cane, and he rose up and frowned awfully. "This my nephew Stephen? Impossible!" I heard this much, and got out as fast as my feet would take me. To think that *he* of all men should catch me at that unlucky sport! (*Stamps round the stage with energy.*)

M. I've told you often that you would get into trouble, Steve. But I did not finish. Uncle Parker has bought a beautiful house, and we are to live with him. Oh! I am so glad mother will have a nice home, and time to rest. And only think, Stephen, he is going to send me to college!

S. Well, I know *my* cake is all dough, Mat; but you deserve your good luck, and I'm glad it has come. As for me, I have learned a lesson I shall not forget; henceforth I shall be kind to the poor drunkard, and no one shall have cause to complain of my conduct in the future.

MRS. NELLIE H. BRADLEY.

FAST COLORS.

THREE CHARACTERS.—*Annie, a little girl, is busy painting a box or piece of wood red. Peter has before him a glass containing a liquid the color of beer, into which he dips his pocket-handkerchief. George, an acquaintance.*

ANNIE. How do you get on with your dyeing, Peter?

PETER. I don't get on at all; it don't seem to get very red! How does yours come on, Annie?

A. Oh! I'm getting on famously! I shall soon have the wood all covered with red!

P. How very fond you are of painting, Annie!

A. Yes, and how very fond of dyeing you are, Peter!

P. Oh! I thought red was a nice color for a handkerchief: it won't show the dirt so quick. Mother says I dirty them so fast, and I wanted a red one like grandpa's.

A. And I only thought red would be a nice bright color for *my* work, you see.

(*Enter George.*)

GEORGE. Hallo! Annie, what are you doing?

A. I'm painting; don't you see?

G. And why red, of all colors?

A. Because I consider it a very *fast* color.

G. And why do you think it is particularly "fast"?

A. Because Deacon Smith's nose is red, and his color never washes out; mother says it never will!

G. That is because he swallows so much rum, Annie!

A. Yes; and my mother says she once knew a little boy who was on board a vessel during a storm!

G. Well, and what of that?

A. Why, he was laughing outright, whilst everybody else expected the vessel would go down every moment.

G. That was curious conduct!

A. Yes, so said the mate; and after the storm was over, he went to the boy, and asked him what he meant by such giggling—at such a time, too!

G. And what did the boy answer?

A. Why, the mate had a very red nose, and the little boy, looking at him, said, "Please, sir, I was just thinking what a *fizz* your nose would make if we were all drowned, and it once touched the water!"

G. Ha! ha! very good! And it is to be hoped that the lesson did the mate some good.

P. Yes, because red noses only come by drinking, 'cause I heard that at the Band of Hope meeting.

G. And pray what are you doing, Peter? I can easily understand Annie; but what in the world is the use of your continually dipping your handkerchief in the glass before you?

P. Oh! it's a good deal of use, I can tell you.

G. And what have you got in the glass?

P. Oh! I've got a good half-pint of beer.

G. Beer? Dear me! Why, you surprise me! Are you not a member of the Band of Hope?

P. Of course I am! I've got a pledge, bless you!

G. Bless *you* as well, then! But what is your object in dipping all the time, Peter?

P. I want to dye this handkerchief red!

G. With beer? Why, it can't be done, child!

P. But it is done sometimes, I know!

G. Dye red by the aid of beer?

P. Yes, sir, look at the drunkard's face!

G. Well, that's red enough usually, I must confess!

P. It's red as can be! Now if I can only dye my

handkerchief half so red as his face is, it will be a nice color, won't it?

G. It may be; but you won't be able to do it.

P. It looks very likely. But the dye is weak, I fear!

G. It is for *that* purpose; for the *other* purpose it is so strong that it has killed thousands of men who had almost the strength of a Samson.

P. Then you think beer won't dye my handkerchief red?

G. I'm certain of it! But I'm glad both of you know the effects of intoxicating drinks; certainly upon the human face they do produce "fast colors"!

Buy Your Own Goose.

CHARACTERS.—*Landlord, Eli Baxter, John Mason, Mrs. Baxter and two Daughters; John Case, errand-boy; Marketman or grocer's messenger.*

LANDLORD. Let's see; it's just four weeks to Christmas. What do you say, gentlemen, to another Goose Club?

MASON. All right! How will you work it?

L. Well, each member will pay ten cents a day, and the twentieth day will draw a fine fat goose and a bottle of gin. Here's the paper. I'd be glad to get your names to head the list. What say *you*, Mr. Baxter?

BAXTER. I guess you must count me out this time, landlord. I'm thinking I've been in the goose business long enough.

M. That's rich! Baxter's cut his wisdom teeth all at once.

B. Perhaps it wouldn't harm some others to cut theirs, too. If you join this club, you'll have to come every day to pay the ten cents, and the landlord won't expect you to be so mean as not to "wet your whistle" for the good of the house. You'll pay well for the goose before you eat it, I reckon.

L. Well, Baxter, you needn't interfere with my business. If you don't choose to join, and are so wise and clever all at once, go and buy your own goose.

B. I'll take your advice. So not another drop this side of Christmas.

L. As you like; but don't come meddling with me. Indeed, the quicker you're gone, the better.

B. (*rising to go*). Rather short with as good a customer as I have been! Look, boys, landlord don't care a fig for us, so he can *pluck* us to feather his own nest. But he sha'n't pluck *me*. I'll take his good advice instead of grog, and "buy my own goose."

SCENE II.

(*In Baxter's house. Mother and two Daughters, Jane and Emma, in pinching poverty.*)

JANE. Ah! mother, I don't want to go to school any more.

MOTHER. Why not, my child?

J. The girls keep talking about Christmas and what good times they will have. They expect nice presents and such good dinners, turkeys, pies, and cakes. It made my mouth water to hear of them. I couldn't help crying to think of our home, and then I heard Mary Grey whisper, "Poor thing! her father's a drunkard, and spends his money at the tavern, and her poor mother can't give her any good things." I don't want to go to school again.

EMMA. Nor I. But why can't we have a pudding this year? We did last. Oh! it was so good.

M. Last year I had work. But good Mrs. Ward is gone, and I can't get my dear girls a Christmas dinner this year.

J. Why will father drink so much and spend his money so?

M. I think he would leave off if the tavern-keeper did not keep enticing him on. The man gets up clubs and dances, and then calls father mean if he won't join. Last year he got up a goose club. Each man paid ten cents every day, and at the end of twenty days was to have a goose; but when the time came, father owed more than the goose was worth, and the man kept it for his pay. If the grog-shop could be shut up, I could hope that my dear girls could have a merry Christmas again, and a dear father too.

SCENE III.

(*Baxter in the street, carrying a basket.*)

B. (*to himself*). It's awkward carrying this basket myself. The fact is, I have not done the fair thing by poor Lizzie and the children. If I can find a boy, I'll play a little trick. Well, sure enough, there comes John Case. He's a trusty fellow. Hallo! John, just come over here.

JOHN. What's up now, Mr. Baxter?

B. Well, you see, I haven't been in the habit of carrying home such baskets as this, and it's awkward business to begin. But now I haven't been to the tavern for four weeks, so I've just bought a fine goose, with flour, sugar, tea, and all the fixings. Here's ten cents. Just take this basket to No. 6, opposite the third lamp-post yonder. Say it's for Mrs. Baxter, and if she won't take it in, drop it at her feet, and run back. If you'll do it up clever, I'll give you ten cents more. (*Boy runs.*)

B. (*to himself*). I'll just peek a little. There, she won't take it. Poor Lizzie! she thinks there's nothing good for her. I've been a wretch! God helping me, I'll fill that woman's heart with joy again before I die. There, he's coming.

J. She said it wasn't for her, and told me to go to another Baxter's, round the corner. But I said I wasn't going to run all over the parish, and dropped the basket.

B. Well done! There's your money.

J. Thank you, sir. I'll buy a Christmas toy for sissie Jane.

Scene IV.

(*Baxter's home. Wife and Girls as before.*)

Jane. If only we could have such a basket!

Emma. There, father's coming. I hear his steps. (*Comes in, hits his foot against the basket in the entry.*)

Baxter. What's here for folks to stumble over?

Mrs. B. A boy left a basket here by mistake. I told him it wasn't for us, but the heedless fellow bolted off.

B. What's in it?

J. Oh! a fine, fat goose, and lots of good things.

E. Why can't we have such things, father? Mother says we have nothing for Christmas.

J. There, somebody knocks.

Mrs. B. Hush! Let me go to the door.

Marketman. Is this Mrs. Eli Baxter?

Mrs. B. Yes.

M. Here is a lot of apples and vegetables for you.

Mrs. B. There's some mistake; they are not for me.

M. Here 'tis on this paper—Mrs. Eli Baxter, No. 6 Poverty Lane.

Mrs. B. Well, now, our house must be bewitched to-night.

B. (*calls out*). Bring them in, sir. Take all that comes, I say. (*Marketman goes.*)

Mrs. B. What can it all mean?

B. It means a merry Christmas, Lizzie, for you and me and the girls. I haven't done as I should by you and the girls; but four weeks ago I signed the pledge; since then not a drop for liquor, but all for you. Here, it is all paid for. There's ten dollars besides. Forgive me, if you can, and pray for me, and hereafter I'll buy my own goose instead of the landlord's.

THE PUMP AND THE TAVERN

CHARACTERS.—*Pump, Tavern, Drunkard's Wife, Public Opinion, Legislation.*

PUMP. My name is Pump. There is nothing extraordinary in my appearance, it is true: neither is there anything very elegant in my structure; but this I may say of myself: I am a useful member of society; I am the friend of every man, woman, and child; the very dogs in the street regard me as their benefactor. I said I was useful. Well, it would require the tongue of a lawyer and the eloquence of an orator justly to describe in how many ways I am serviceable. I am used in public and private, in summer and in winter, by people of every rank and condition in life. There is not a branch of industry, or a department in science or art, with which I am not directly or indirectly connected. Where would be the world-famed cotton and woolen fabrics, were I not to assist in the bleaching and dyeing processes? Where would be the extensive traffic on our railways, were not my element forced into the locomotive-boiler and generated into steam? Where would be all the treasures of literature, were I not to assist in the manufacture of paper? Where would be all the necessaries and luxuries of life, were not my element to descend in fertilizing showers upon waving corn-fields and teeming orchards? Where would be all the beauties and charms of nature, the colors of the rainbow, the perfume and tints of flowers, the warbling of birds, the splendor of landscape; in short, what would be the— [*Enter Tavern.*]

TAVERN. Oh! ah! yes! How are you, Mr. Pump? Haven't seen you I don't care when. (*Attempts to shake hands.*)

P. No, no; let every rogue shake his own hand.

T. (*tries again*). Shake hands, old fellow, with your friend, Mr. Tavern.

P. Friend! How can I recognize a friend in one of the greatest foes to human happiness? You are the prolific source of crime, pauperism, insanity, and death; you are the enemy of the church and the Sabbath-school; you hinder every benevolent and philanthropic movement; you retard all intellectual, social, and moral advancement; you are—

T. Stay, stay; I cannot, I will not suffer you thus to insult me.

P. You are the—

T. I tell you I cannot let you proceed further until you hear me vindicate my character. I have been impeached most unjustly by young and old in these modern times. Now, I mean to say that I am a public benefactor [*a voice cries "Public nuisance!"*]. What was that, Mr. Pump?

P. Why, the very boys in the street are calling you a public nuisance.

T. I suppose these are some of your Band of Hope friends. Why don't you teach them to respect their superiors?

(*Enter Drunkard's Wife.*)

DRUNKARD'S WIFE. Respect you! Who can respect those who take the bread out of the children's mouths and the clothes from their backs?

T. Do I ask your husband to spend his money with me?

D. W. No, Mr. Tavern, but you do far worse; you insinuate that you are his friend.

T. Of course I am!

P. Let the poor woman speak.

D. W. You allure him with gilded rooms and fine music; but who will compensate me for the injury I sustain from you?

T. If your husband is fool enough to spend his money with me, all I can say is—that—ah!—

P. That he *is* a fool.

T. Did I call her husband a fool?

D. W. Yes, you did (*sobs*); I heard you.

T. Well, I beg your pardon; I meant to say that—ah!—

P. The fact is, you can say nothing in your own defence, for so long as you are allowed to exist these direful consequences must follow; but let me warn you that all my temperance friends are now combined for your entire suppression and overthrow.

T. My overthrow! Ha! ha! How absurd to talk about demolishing one of the oldest, the strongest, the most elegant, useful, and benevolent institutions in the country!

D. W. Benevolent! For shame, sir!

T. Do I not furnish a spacious room for your husband's comfort? Do I not seek to refine his taste by exhibiting on my walls the paintings of great artists? Do I not endeavor to dispel his sorrow and brighten his imagination with classical music, both vocal and instrumental, not to mention the dazzling splendor of my mirrors and chandeliers? Can you offer such good things for your husband at his own home?

D. W. God knows I cannot while he leaves his money with you, Mr. Tavern. (*Goes out crying.*)

T. I cannot tell what that woman is crying for.

P. Ah! if you could witness all the desolate homes, the starving children, and broken-hearted mothers, made so by you, you would understand what she is crying for.

T. Have I not said that I do not compel people to enter my house? If people will drink until reason is dethroned, until the ties of nature and affection are severed, and the body laid prostrate in disease and wretchedness, what is it to me? It is their own deliberate act.

(*Enter Public Opinion.*)

PUBLIC OPINION. My name is Public Opinion. I have been reflecting upon the services which you two gentlemen render to my country. You, Mr. Pump, have my entire approbation; you daily and hourly contribute to the happiness and prosperity of my people. Your element sweeps in the foaming ocean, and bears upon its bosom the wealth of nations. Your element circulates in clouds, and descends in showers that fertilize the soil and invigorate all vegetable life. Without your element the luxuries and necessaries of life could not be produced, no process of manufacture completed, no result in science or art obtained; in short, Mr. Pump, life itself would become extinct and creation a blank were it not for your element. You have been a faithful old friend; henceforth your name shall be Fountain. You shall stand in the most fashionable and public streets and squares in my country. You shall have a most elegant appearance, and all my people shall regard you as a public benefactor.

P. I am flattered by the compliment, sir.

T. Have you not one word of commendation for me, Mr. Public Opinion?

P. O. You! you heartless villain! You, whose hand is against every man! You, the betrayer of my children, the foe of commerce, the enemy of social and religious progress, the distributer of crime, disease, poverty, insanity, and death! I have been a long time trying to restrain you with gentle measures, but to no purpose. Every day I learn from my friend, the public press, that your outrages upon society are more frequent and more violent than ever. My mind is fully made up!

T. Spare me! spare me! Mr. Public Opinion.

P. O. Not for another day. I will call in my officer at

once, and order your execution. (*Calls in a loud voice for Legislation.*)

[*Enter Legislation.*]

P. O. Officer, this person must be taken to the jail. I will sign his death-warrant at six o'clock to-day. No further trial is needed. My voice is law. Seize him, and do your duty!

(*L. seizes him by the collar, and drags him off. Exit.*)

INDEPENDENCE.

CHARACTERS.—*Susie and Nellie.*

SUSIE. Then you would really wish to deprive all young men of a social glass of wine, and bind them down to the contracted limits of a temperance pledge?

NELLIE. I do wish to see *all* our young men and women become pledged to total abstinence. I do not think any one safe while indulging even in wine-drinking. I know many who drank good wine a few years ago that now drink poor whiskey.

S. Oh! I have no patience with whiskey-drinkers, but I do like to see young men independent, and *dare* to take a glass of wine when they wish to. What would the eagle say to having his wings clipped?

N. I saw one of your independent young men this morning; but, with all his independence, he was unable to arise from the gutter (into which he had fallen) without assistance.

S. That was shocking! He was no doubt a miserable drunkard, which is altogether different from merely taking a glass of wine. You know that wine has been used by all, or nearly all, of our best men, the greatest names in our country's history. You recollect what the poet says,

"Drink till the moon goes down."

N. I think it would be an improvement to say, Drink till themselves go down.

S. Oh! I see this temperance whirlwind has turned your brain; you will come to your senses by-and-by, and learn that a young man is something less than a murderer if he does drink a glass of wine now and then. There is but a small chance of your ever getting a husband, if harmless wine-drinking is to prove an obstacle.

N. Neither do I wish to get one with the first step taken to the drunkard's grave. Would you cross the Atlantic if you were told the noble ship in which you were to sail was known to be a little leaky, but might carry you safely to old England's shore? Would you not prefer to always stay at home rather than trust your life to a treacherous craft that might, before you had half reached your journey's end, sink you beneath the boiling wave? No, never will I unite my destiny with one who is in the habit of drinking wine. Total abstinence or no husband is my motto.

S. I am sure I do not want a drunkard for a husband; and if I thought that he would ever drink anything stronger than wine, I would use all my influence to induce him to sign the pledge, and keep it too.

N. Oh! do use your influence in persuading all to join the Lodge or Division; there is no safety elsewhere. Show by your own example that your heart is in the cause, and that wine-bibbing finds no favor in your eyes.

S. But you really do not think I am in danger? I never drank a glass of wine in my life. Would you have me join the division, and mix my name with the low and degraded?

N. No false pride should prevent us from doing our duty, neither should we refuse to aid a reforming movement simply because it will not benefit us. Let us use all our influence, speak boldly and fearlessly when occasion requires us to do so. Our brothers are in danger;

our dear friends are in danger; and we are in danger. Let us not deal with the arrows of death, lest those arrows pierce our own hearts at last.

S. Why, you alarm me; everything seems to be intoxicated that I look at; every post, pillar, man, and beast has a zigzag motion. I will fly into the ark of safety, join your division, and adopt your motto.

DIALOGUE ON USING TOBACCO.

CHARACTERS.—*Joseph and Samuel.*

JOSEPH. Hallo, Sam! where now?

SAMUEL. I'm going down to the Common to play ball. Don't you want to go?

J. Yes; I've done my stint, and father says I may now go where I please.

S. Give me a chew of tobacco, Joe.

J. Tobacco! I haven't any; I don't use it.

S. Don't use it? What a fool! You'll not be a man till you do.

J. I shall not be a man if I do, that's certain. Who advised you to use it?

S. Jim Sanders.

J. Jim Sanders? I'm sorry you wish to follow his example.

S. Why?

J. Jim Sanders, you know, is a worthless fellow. He uses profane language, seeks mean company, and spends his evenings at grog-shops, when he ought to be at home at work or perusing his books. Do your parents allow you to use tobacco?

S. No; Jim Sanders worked for father a great part of the time during the last two years. He said I should never be a man till I had learned to chew tobacco. He has supplied me with it till now. When I commenced using it, it made me sick; I would vomit freely. Now I can chew it freely nearly all the time.

J. Do your parents know it?

S. No.

J. How can you deceive them?

S. Jim supplies me with cloves. After chewing tobacco, I chew *them;* they take away the scent. Jim has left town for good. I am out of tobacco. I have no money and no chance to earn any to buy with. I don't want to ask father for any, because I shall be obliged to tell him what I want of it.

J. Can you sincerely say you love it?

S. No.

J. Do you think you can abstain from it?

S. Yes.

J. Then do it. Which do you consider the most respectable, Mr. Clark or Jim Sanders?

S. Mr. Clark, to be sure.

J. Mr. Clark, you know, is a gentleman. He never used tobacco; he greatly abhors it. It is used most freely by the base, illiterate class. The more you use it, the harder it will be to abstain from it. Break off now, by all means. It is a very low, filthy habit. Above all, avoid mean company.

S. I will. I was deceived. You have convinced me of it. I am greatly obliged to you. No one knows I ever used tobacco but you and Jim Sanders. Don't tell anybody, I beg of you.

J. Certainly not. I trust you will keep your promise faithfully. May I not hope you will be a temperate, steady, useful man?

DAVID W. WELCH.

Learning to Smoke.

CHARACTERS.—*Herbert, sitting in a chair with a partly-smoked cigar hanging down at his side. Enter Clark.*

CLARK. Hallo, Bert! what are you doing up here in the dumps? There's a capital wind for kiting. Come and help me put up my Old Abe. I've got him in splendid trim. I've been mending his wings, and sticking some new feathers in his tail, and I want to put him up from your roof.

HERBERT (*feebly*). Well, nobody's any objections.

C. What's the matter with you—sick? Turn around to the light, here. (*Wheeling him about, facing the audience, while Herbert quietly drops his cigar.*) Pale as a ghost, I declare! What have you been doing?

H. Nothing. But I don't feel quite right, that's a fact.

C. Well, you look as flat as if you'd been learning to smoke tobacco, and (*snuffing the air*) I think I smell it. Come now, own up. You've been smoking.

H. Oh! nonsense.

C. Yes, "nonsense"; but you don't deny it. That's pretty business; poisoning yourself with that filthy stuff, and making yourself a monkey of a mimic!

H. A monkey, indeed! What are you talking about? You'd better prove your charges before you get up such a lecture as that.

C. A good smell will prove it, I dare say. (*Stoops, as if to smell of him, when he spies the cigar, and pounces upon it.*) Ah! here's the proof. What do you say to that? (*Herbert looks confused, and hangs his head.*) Confess guilty, eh? And hiding it, and denying it, too! Well, now, Bertie, that uses me up! I never thought that of you. (*A pause.*) I always thought you the very soul of honor.

I'd have taken your word before that of any other boy in school. And here *you* are quibbling about *tobacco!* Why I'd have knocked a boy down that would have told me that of you.

H. Why, now, what is there so awful about it?

C. Will you tell me, Bertie, what made you try to hide it, if it wasn't bad? (*A pause, but no reply.*) I suppose, now (*gently*), you wouldn't want your father to know it, nor your Sunday-school teacher, would you?

H. No, Clark, I can't say that I would; and yet it was because I saw them sitting and smoking together so cosy Sunday afternoon that made me wish to smoke too.

C. Did you ask them to teach you?

H. Why, no! What a ridiculous idea!

C. Why, if it's a good thing to use tobacco, and everybody knows it's so difficult to learn, who would be a more proper person to teach you than your own father or your Sunday-school teacher?

H. Well, I wouldn't like to ask them, any how.

C. That shows there's something wrong about it.

H. What is it, then? They're good men. They ought to do right.

C. Well, I don't quite know, Bertie; but I think good men don't always do right in all things. They used to drink, you know, before the temperance reform, ministers and all—before they knew how much it hurt them.

H. But people know about tobacco, don't they?

C. Some do, and some don't. It seems you didn't know enough to keep you from trying it. But you see they learn it slyly when they're boys, just as you began it here; and so no one warned them till it was done, and they first begin to think when the habit is so fixed that they cannot shake it off without a great struggle. Sometimes it makes them much sicker than it did to learn.

H. Why, I didn't know that. John Decker says he can give it up any time.

C. Well, he'd better do it, then, before he gets to be as bad as his brother Henry. It's killing him, and he knows it; but when he tries to leave it off, it gives him the real *tremens.*

H. Whew! Well, I *would* stop before I got so bad as that.

C. I tell you the only safe way is to stop before you begin, and then you don't have any trouble about it. There's many an old tobacco-chewer that would give lots of money if he was just back where you are, and he'd take the pledge against it mighty quick.

H. The pledge?

C. Yes; I've got one here in a pledge-book (*pulling it out of his pocket*). I've put my name to it, and I'd just like to have yours right under it.

H. (*takes it and reads*). Never to take tobacco in any shape as long as I live. Well, I may as well now as ever.

C. Here's a pencil.

H. (*signs his name*). So here's a good-by to falsehoods and dodgings, and I hope you'll trust me for a truth-teller from this time out.

C. That I will. (*They shake hands*). And now I want to get all the boys I can to sign this, and perhaps we can get up a society.

H. What, a society against smoking?

C. Yes, against tobacco in every shape—something like the Good Templars against alcohol. And we could take the boys that are too young to go to the Good Templars, and perhaps the girls would come in too.

H. Good! I go in for that. Let's go and get Chris Howland; I guess he'll help. (*They go off together.*)

JULIA COLMAN.

TAKING A STAND.

CHARACTERS.—*Ralph and Edward.*

RALPH. Don't you think our teacher is a *little* particular, Ed? I don't believe I'll join the Band, for I *know* I can be a good proof that it isn't necessary.

EDWARD. I don't think he's *too* particular at all. Suppose *you* could stand, as proof; it isn't every one that *can;* and I'm willing to stand for the sake of helping *others* stand, if need be.

R. I don't see the harm, any way, in a little pure wine now and then—a mere taste at a party, or when handed you by a friend.

E. Not "seeing the harm" is the worst rock to split on there is. It's a little, low rock, without any lighthouse a-top, or any bell-buoy beside it; and many a ship has struck there, after going safely past worse dangers, where they were pointed out. Tim Carson is in his grave to-day, because *he* "didn't see any harm" in a little wine on New Year's day. It came so many times, and tasted so good each time, that the habit was formed which he never broke afterward.

R. Tim never had much force, any way.

E. I don't know about that. You'll admit Joe Ellsler *had,* and he hung himself before he had "seen the harm" many days.

R. Oh! well, that was a peculiar case. It wouldn't happen once in a thousand times. Joe was *mortified to death* because he *happened* to get drunk, and the fellows led him into mischief, and he couldn't stand the disgrace of having to be expelled.

E. Perhaps it was a peculiar case, but it saved Robert White; and I heard Rob say he'd give a thousand dollars if he hadn't laughed poor Joe out of signing the pledge one day last winter, when the boys first got it up.

R. Well he might, *as things turned out.*

E. We never can tell how things are *going* to turn out. That's it; and if I'm safe myself, I shall do all I can to help save others. Every paper you take up is full of murders, and suicides, and terrible cruelties, all started by rum, and yet nobody can "see the harm," or where it lies. I think it's proof enough of what comes from having no fear of a *little* wine. There's a world-wide difference in not beginning, and stopping after you've once started. A precious few can stop when they choose; but with most who begin to run on a down grade, they never stop till they reach the bottom.

KRUNA.

THE MOTTO OF OUR ORDER.

(*To be performed by three little girls, representing Love, Purity, and Fidelity, and wearing dresses or sashes of the appropriate colors—the red, white, and blue—also small crowns, each having a star in the centre.*

Love.

O RUM! thou dark monster, how gloomy thy reign!
What tears have been shed o'er thy millions of slain!
What hopes thou hast wrecked, what sad trophies won!
Thou hast slain the fond father, and smitten the son.

Purity.

Thou hast entered the mansion, and hung it with gloom,
Thou hast dug for bright genius a premature tomb;

The learned thou hast conquered, the gifted o'er-
thrown,
The eloquent stricken—claimed *all* as thine own.

Fidelity.

Bright homes thou hast darkened, and 'neath *thy* sad
tread
Our loved ones have fallen, and sleep with the dead;
The husband, the father, the brother, the son,
Thy cup has destroyed—they have gone one by one.

Love.

I come from the councils of the blest, on a mission to the children of men. I visit the sick, lift up the fainting head, and cheer the failing heart. I watch by the bedside of the suffering, smooth the pillow of the dying, and whisper words of everlasting life. This is my mission. *I* am LOVE.

Purity.

I show the sons of men how to be spotless in heart and life; for in that beautiful land of ineffable glory to which our Father will call his ransomed ones, no stain of sin, no shadowy cloud of earth, shall dim the heavenly radiance. I teach all to shun evil and guile, and to love that which is good and pure. My name is PURITY.

Fidelity.

I teach the children of earth to have faith in God, and to be true to each other. The world is full of sin and misery, because they transgress the laws of God. I show them how faithful are his promises, and that in keeping his commandments there is great reward. This is my mission. I am FIDELITY.

Purity (with clasped hands).

O God of the widow! the orphan's last friend,
Whose conquering kingdom shall ne'er know an end,
Swift speed the glad day when rum's reign shall be o'er,
And *our* trio of virtues [*all join hands*] shall bind shore to shore;
When the last tear shall fall o'er the spoils it has won,
When the last wretched father, the last reeling son,
Shall stand 'neath the banner of temperance unfurled,
And the song of the victors shall ring through the world.
Then the wine-cup shall shatter, the dragon be chained,
The curse shall be banished, the heart no more pained,
And the bright crystal waters our Father has given
Shall be man's only drink as he passes to heaven.

All Sing.

Then up with the temperance banner!
  Its proud motto give to the sun,
May our faith in our cause never wither,
  Nor cease till the victory is won.
May Purity, Fidelity, Love, ever
  Inspire us our pledge to renew,
Our Cause and our Order for ever—
  Three cheers for the red, white, and blue!

Three cheers for the red, white, and blue,
Three cheers for the red, white, and blue!
  Our glorious Order for ever,
Three cheers for the red, white, and blue!

(*An invisible quartet placed near the trio, and joining in the chorus of the song, adds greatly to the effect.*)

Arranged by MRS. NELLIE H. BRADLEY.

TEMPERANCE ALPHABET.

(*To make this more effective and pleasing, it should be recited by twenty-six small boys or girls, each representing a letter.*)

A stands for Ale, a most poisonous drink;
People are foolish who taste it, I think.

B stands for Beer, that's as bad, if not worse;
Both prove to the drinker a ruin and curse.

C stands for Cider; don't sip it, I pray,
For many a drunkard is made in that way.

D stands for Drop; though but one's in the cup,
A bowlful may follow if you drink it up.

E stands for Earnings; and many a man
Spends his in the beer-shop—a very poor plan.

F stands for Fiend; and the worst fiend of all
Is the many-faced demon, old Alcohol.

G stands for Gutter, a wretched mud-hole,
Where men oft lie down who imbibe from the bowl.

H stands for Horror the drunken man feels,
When, with "snakes in his boots," he staggers and reels.

I stands for Ills, with pains, poverty, woes,
That Alcohol carries wherever he goes.

J stands for Justice; a good thing, no doubt,
Which the judge who drinks liquor knows nothing about.

K stands for Kindness; a word which, I fear,
The men who sell liquor are too deaf to hear.

L stands for Lying; strong drink is a foe
To truth and to honor, as all people know.

M stands for Mourning; all over our land
Alcohol makes it with his cruel band.

N stands for Nobles; true nobles are they
Who battle this demon by night and by day.

O stands for Odious, which people become
When they make themselves barrels for brandy and rum.

P stands for Peace, which is certain to fly
When riotous alcohol's huts are near by.

Q stands for Quantity; little or much,
Strong drink is a thing you had better not touch.

R stands for Rowdy, Rumseller, and Riot;
Prohibition will give them all three a new diet.

S stands for Silly; the drunkard is that
When he goes reeling home with a brick in his hat.

T stands for Trials, that make up the life
Of the drunkard's poor children and sad-hearted wife.

U stands for Use; it's a very good word,
But the use of strong liquors is simply absurd.

V stands, I suppose, for the harmless grape-vine;
God gave us the fruit, but men make the wine,

W stands for Wickedness, Wailing, and Woes;
They are all in the wine-cup the drunkard well knows

X stands for—well, really, I do not know what,
But it crosses its legs like a drunken old sot.

Y stands for Yield, and old Alcohol must,
For we soldiers will humble him down in the dust.

Z stands for Zero—zero for naught,
Naught (o) stands for nothing;
And that is just what
Boys find in their pockets who tipple and drink;
It's a very bad habit, I certainly think.

ELLA WHEELER.

CIDER DRINKING.

CHARACTERS.—*Farmer Drew, Bessie Drew, Johnny Lane, Frank Perkins.*

SCENE—*The Farmer's Kitchen. Farmer Drew sitting in a big chair. Bessie sitting by the table, with one arm in a sling, reading aloud from a newspaper. On the table are a pitcher of cider and mugs.*

BESSIE (*reading*). "Why, now, is President Johnson impeached? Simply because—" Oh! dear, papa, I am so tired of this impeachment question! I do wish he would come! I want you to see him so much?

FARMER. Who? President Johnson? Well, now, I an't at all partic'lar about seein' him. I'd a good deal sooner hear you read about him, that's a fact.

B. Now, papa, I think you are too bad! You know I didn't mean President Johnson.

FAR. How should I know? He was the only "him" you was readin' about, anyhow.

B. Well, I meant the little candy merchant that saved my life the other day. O papa! Dr. Frost said if he hadn't rushed up and pulled me right out from under that horse's feet, I should have been killed on the spot!

FAR. Noble little fellow! I do want to see him, Bessie,

and I wish I could do something for him. The doctor says they are as poor as poverty.

B. Yes, papa, and he's got a little sister, and he keeps her and their mother by selling candy. We'll buy him out, won't we, papa?

FAR. I don't know about that. I'm afraid you've got a sweet tooth somewhere, pussy-cat! (*Turning out some cider, and offering it to Bessie.*) Here, child, wet your whistle, and read some more about "Andrew."

B. No, papa, I can't bear the sour stuff. It makes me make up a face to see you drink it. Ugh! how can you?

FAR. That's because you've got a sweet tooth. I don't know about that little candy merchant coming here so much. You used to like a drink of good cider with your old father.

B. Well, papa, I am never going to drink any more, you see, and I guess Cousin Frank won't either! O papa! there's Johnny Lane now, and Frank is with him. (*Runs to meet them.*)

[*Enter Johnny with his candy-tray, accompanied by Frank.*]

F. Uncle Drew, this is the little candy boy that saved Bessie.

FAR. Do come here, and shake hands with the old farmer, youngster; that was a brave thing you did, boy, and I can never thank you enough!

J. Oh! that was nothing much. I never stopped to think; I just sprung up, and hit the horse a lounder, and grabbed the little girl—that wasn't much!

FAR. Well, I think 'twas real brave and noble, and you won't lose nothing, now I can tell you. But you look cold, both of you. 'Tis a plaguy cold night for the first of April; here (*turning out the cider into mugs, and offering it to the boys*), take a good swig of cider, both of ye. 'Twill do you good.

J. No, sir, thank you; I don't like to drink cider.

FAR. Don't like cider? But you will like *my* cider, I

know. I made it myself out o' some of my best baldwins, and it's nice—jest a leetle hard, but that don't hurt it a grain. Try a leetle on't, boys.

J. No, sir, I cannot. I do like the taste of cider, but I've signed the pledge, and I cannot take anything that will intoxicate, not even cider.

FAR. Well, that's smart! I've taken cider every day for nigh on to forty years, and I never was intosticated in my life. I'm near about mad that you should insinuate such a thing.

B. (*laughing*). O papa! you said the funniest word!

FAR. Well 'tan't 'cause I don't know better, but my tongue is kinder thick, child, and I never could quite get the hang of that big word. But as for cider bein' intosti—there it is again—intosti-toxticating, you see I don't b'lieve in it, I don't.

J. I didn't mean any offence, sir; I beg your pardon!

FAR. Oh! no offence, youngster. You saved little Bessie, and I couldn't get out with *you*, no how. But I s'pose your father's one o' these strict temperance folks, and you don't know better.

J. My father is dead. He died two years ago. He wasn't a temperance man at all. I wish he had been.

FAR. What did he die of? Not of drink, did he?

J. Yes, sir! And mother says he began by drinking beer and cider when he was a young man.

F. (*snatching up the mug, and drinking the cider at a draught*). There! that's what *I* think about it—prime old cider that, Uncle Drew!

FAR. Well, Frank Perkins, for a boy o' your years, I must say that's going it rather steep!

B. O Frank! how could you?

F. Why, Uncle Drew, you said it was good for us, and I like it, I do! Tell you what, such a mug o' cider's that'll set a fellow up! It goes to the right spot.

B. O Frank! how *could* you drink it?

F. How could I? Why, I just opened my mouth *so*

(*taking up the other mug*), and tipped the mug up *so*, and—

FAR. (*taking the mug from him*). No you don't! not in my house, young man!

F. (*scratching his head*). Well, I didn't, did I? But, Bess, that's the way I could do it, if I wasn't hindered. It is *just as easy!*

J. Are you crazy, Frank Perkins?

F. Why, you all look as if I'd done something horrid! Do you think I'll be a drunkard any sooner for taking a mug of cider?

J. Yes, I do. I think every mug of cider you drink, you will be the more likely to become a drunkard.

FAR. N-no, don't know's I *do*. But it startled me a leetle to see a small shaver like you gobblin' down sich a big mugful—and hard cider, too.

F. Well, I drank three the other day before we went a-coasting; and, uncle, *you* told me 'twould do me good. I've got so I can carry off two very well, but that third mugful was a leetle *too* much.

B. Papa, Dr. Frost says Frank was real dizzy, and it was the cider made him steer my sled off the bank.

FAR. Child! child! what do you mean?

J. Frank was real tight, Mr. Drew—he'll tell you so himself—*on your cider!*

F. Only boozy, uncle, so I saw two objects for one, and the ground kept coming up and hitting me in the face, and that's what sent little Bessie flying over the bank right in the midst of all those horses and sleighs.

B. Yes, papa, and *you* coaxed him to drink it—I heard you. You said, " 'Twill do you good, Frank! 'Twill keep out the cold, Frank!" Now, papa, if Frank had killed me, *he* wouldn't have been to blame, don't you see?

FAR. Yes, I see, child; I should have been your murderer—that's so! Well, I'll never ask you to take a mug of cider again, Frank, that's a fact.

B. Nor me, papa?

FAR. No, nor you, puss! I'll take my cider by myself in future.

B. I wish you wouldn't take it at all, papa. Frank, you're going to sign the pledge, aren't you? Please, Frankie! If you don't, I'll never forgive you for throwing me to the horses and breaking my arm.

FAR. I think you'd better, boy. Why, if I'd a gone and drunk sich a mug o' cider as that 'ere at *your* age, I'd a been a gutter-drunkard now!

J. Come, Frank, join our Band of Hope. We do have the jolliest times!

F. No, I won't do it! But I'll tell you what I *will* do, uncle. I'm rather too big and lubberly to go with those children. But I'll jine the Good Templar's Lodge, if you will, uncle. Come, now, what do you say?

FAR. Me! Jine the lodge, and give up my mug o' cider o' nights, and be a reg'lar teetotaler? Why, boys, I should dry up and blow away in a month! No smokin' allowed, I 'spose! No tea nor coffee allowed either, I 'spose!

B. Oh! yes, uncle; the Good Templars smoke like a steam-engine, some of them, and chew like fun—more shame for them! And tea and coffee are allowed always. O papa! I have learned to make a "royal" cup of tea.

FAR. (*taking out his memorandum-book and writing*). Well, child, if there's one thing I *do* like better'n cider, it's a royal cup o' tea. (*After writing a moment.*) Well, children, here's my pledge, and you've all on you got to sign it with me. (*Reads.*) "Seein' I've come plaguy nigh makin' a drunkard of my nephew Frank—a harum-scarum, he is, but good as wheat at heart—and seein' how nigh I come to bein' the means o' his murderin' my darlin' by coaxin' him to drink more cider'n was good for him, I do solemnly pledge myself never to buy, or sell, or give away, or drink anything that can intos-ti-toxicate, for ninety-nine years to come. Signed, Ebenezer Drew." Now, youngsters, put your names here.

[*All come up and sign.*]

B. (*dancing round her father*). Now, papa, buy the candy out, and treat us all around.

FAR. Oh! what a sweet tooth that child has got! Well, you all please jine and sing something first, and I'll see—I'll see, child.

[*All sing some appropriate piece.*]

LIKES AND DISLIKES.

CHARACTERS.—*John and Mary.*

JOHN. I should not like a red, red nose.
MARY. That is the color of the rose.
J. The hue for flowers is good enough.
M. So 'tis for noses up to snuff.
J. The toper's nose is ruby red.
M. That is the color of your head.
J. Now, Mate, stop poking fun at me.
M. What a good light-house that would be!
J. Do you refer to my red hair?
M. To anything that burns in air.
J. You pretty, witty, little scold.
M. It is a radiant crown of gold.
J. I should not like a toper's eyes.
M. They are not clear as cloudless skies.
J. They're water-drops in rings of pink.
M. Say drops of rum and blots of ink.
J. I should not like his parched lips.
M. They're water-proof as clipper-ships.
J. But ships sometimes may spring a-leak.
M. The drunkard does—look at his cheek.
J. Our drink is poured in silver showers.
M. For girls and boys, and birds and flowers.

G. W. BUNGAY.

WE WILL STAND BY THE FLAG.

AN acting acrostic for twenty boys, who should each have a letter in the right hand. A sheet of card-board, with a large capital letter plainly printed on, will answer the purpose. As each boy comes out and recites his line, he should hold up the card containing the letter with which his line commences. When all have recited, the motto of the piece can be seen plainly by the letters. At the close, let them recite or sing the verse given below, to the tune of "*Jeannette and Jeannot*." To add to the effect, a large flag should be prettily draped; or they can hold a small flag in the left hand, and wave it as they sing.

W hat though the hill be rough and high,
E xcelsior! shall be our cry.

W hat though the foe be firm and strong,
I f we are right, and he is wrong.
L et's nobly battle for the right;
L et's *win*, or *never cease* to fight!

S hould drinkers frown and proud men sneer,
T hen by our acts we'll show how dear
A nd *good* our cause, by living down
N eglect, abuse, and sneer, and frown—
D efeat comes not, if *we* endure;

B ut victory by-and-by is sure;
Y es, though the foe be linked with sin,

T hough thousands serve and worship him,
H e yet shall fall and bite the dust;
E arth *shall* be pure, for God is just.

F ear not, then, ye who work and pray!
L ong coming, yet there *comes* a day—
A day when drunkenness shall cease,
G od glorified, and man at peace.

All Sing.

(Tune—"*Jeannette and Jeannot.*")

A happy day is coming,
  When King Bacchus shall resign
His throne to pure Queen Temperance,
  And water conquer wine;
And the day will come the sooner,
  If you help the cause along,
And join our band, and not forget,
  The motto of our song.

EDWARD CARSWELL.

THE CROOKED TREE.

CHARACTERS.—*Annie and Sarah*

ANNIE. How very happy you look this morning, Sarah! Something has pleased you, I'm sure.

SARAH. Oh! yes, Annie; father has signed the temperance pledge.

A. Father signed the pledge! How ridiculous! Your father never was a drunkard.

S. No; but he went to hear a temperance sermon.

A. Well, and what of that?

S. Why, father was so convinced that teetotalism was better than drinking that he signed the pledge there and then.

A. What's the use of talking about drinking, when you say your father never was a drunkard?

S. I know that father never was a drunkard, but I must confess that he was a drinker.

A. A drinker! Why, how much did he drink—a gallon a day?

S. No; father used to take a gill at dinner, and another at supper-time.

A. And do you call a man a drinker for that?

S. What do you call him?

A. Why, I'm sure I would not call him a drinker; that would be putting him on the same side as drunkards.

S. What would you call me if you saw me take a glass of water every day?

A. Why, of course, I should call you a water-drinker.

S. But suppose the glass had contained beer instead of water.

A. Why, of course, I should say you were taking your daily glass.

S. What do you mean by taking?

A. Why, you stupid, I mean drinking.

S. Now, come, don't get out of temper, because I want you to call things by their proper names.

A. But I shall never call a man a drinker because he takes a glass now and then. It is shocking to call a good Christian man a drinker; that puts him on the same line as the drunkard!

E. Exactly; that's just what I want to prove. Do you not see that it must be so, since the station of "one glass" is the very place where all drunkards first started?

A. But they must have gone down to a wrong line after.

S. Very true. But don't you see that if they had not started from the station of "one glass," they could never get on the line of drunkenness?

A. I cannot see that.

S. Do you know that crooked tree which grows near Farmer Brownlow's house?

A. Yes; but what has that to do with drinking?

S. Listen. That crooked old tree is just like the drunkard in his crooked and perverse ways, with his ragged coat, his bloodshot eye, and his quivering lip.

A. Yes, I can understand all that.

S. Well, now, how did the tree become so ugly and crooked?

A. Why, because it was not trained properly when it was a tender plant.

S. And that is exactly why people become drunkards—because they were not trained properly while they were young. Don't you remember what the Bible says, "Train up a child in the way he should go; and when he is old, he will not depart from it"? Is that true?

A. Yes, that must be true; for God said it by the mouth of Solomon.

S. Well, now, just think, for a moment, how drunkards are made every year. God sent them into the world, as he sent you and me, perfectly sober, with a body adapted, not for alcohol, but for clear, sparkling water. But when they become boys and girls, and are able to observe and reflect, they see their fathers, and mothers, and friends taking the drink, saying how good and necessary it is for health and happiness, and they believe that what father, and mother, and friends say and do must be right, and thus thousands of boys and girls receive bad impressions and form wrong habits. They begin just to taste a little, and get from little to much, and from much to more, until the full-grown drunkard appears in all his crooked deformity.

A. There is great force in what you say; but I must be off. Good-morning.

S. Stay! There is another thought: are you convinced that teetotalism is right?

A. Oh! yes, I believe it is doing a good work.

S. Then why don't you come and join us?

A. What am I to do?

S. Why, you can do as I do—sign the pledge, and set an example which others may safely follow; and try to get others to sign. You know what the song says,

"Every little mite,
Every little measure,
Helps to spread the light,
Helps to swell the treasure."

A. Yes, you are right; I think I *will* do as you do.

S. Come along, then, and sign the pledge first. (*Annie signs the pledge.*)

W. HOYLE.

THE CHOICE OF TRADES.

(*Eleven boys and girls arranged in a semi-circular group, so as to present their faces in part to the audience, in part towards each other.*)

ONE OF THE LARGER BOYS, *standing near the centre.*

Come, boys and girls,
Let's each of us now
Choose the trade we will have
When we're women and men.
We are all temperance soldiers,
So let what will come,
Our trade sha'n't encourage
The traffic in rum.
Tom Bent, you're the oldest,
We'll begin where *you* stand (*at his right*),
And *I'll* speak after Joseph,
Standing here at this hand (*at his left*).

TOM BENT. *I'll* be a farmer;
But you never shall hear
That Thomas Bent's hops
Ever make lager-beer,
Or that Thomas Bent's apples
Make cider to drink—
For vinegar and cooking
He'll have plenty, I think.
And I'll raise such fine crops
To make men grow strong;
I shall just sing and whistle
The summer day long.

SECOND BOY. *I'll* be a lawyer;
But I never will lend
My counsel to bad men,
A bad cause to defend.
And I'll work without fees
If I ever can aid
The cold-water army
To put down the rum trade.

GIRL. *I'll* be a dressmaker
And milliner too;
My dresses and bonnets
Will be wonders to view.
And I'll do what *I* can
That they never shall hide
The sorrowful heart
Of a rum-drinker's bride.

BOY OR GIRL. *I'll* be a school-teacher,
And shall do what I can
To make of each lad
A good temperance man.
And I'll teach all my girls
To regard with a frown
Both tobacco and rum,
And so put them down.

GIRL OR BOY. *I'll* be a missionary
When I've grown good and wise,
And teach the dark pagans
The way to the skies.
I shall tell them the path
That by drunkards is trod
Leads far, far away
From our Father and God.

BOY. *I'll* be a sailor,
Then captain, some day,
And sail o'er the ocean
To lands far away.
But old Alcohol never
Shall step on *my* deck,
For where'er *he* is harbored
There's sure to be wreck.

BOY. *I'll* be a doctor;
And when folks are ill,
I'll be ready to cure them
With powder or pill.
But I ne'er will prescribe
Whiskey, brandy, or gin,
To awaken old tastes,
Or the new to begin.

GIRL. I'll be a housekeeper,
To broil, bake, and stew,
And take care of my house
As our mothers do.
I'll look after my household,
And ever despise
Putting wine on the table
Or brandy in pies.

BOY. *I'll* be a merchant,
And keep a big store,
With large piles of goods
And clerks by the score.
And I'll pay better wages
Than other men do,
If they'll all be teetotalers,
Tried men and true.

JOSEPH (*at the left hand*). *I* mean to fill
An editor's station,
For *his* words reach men's ears
All over the nation.
I'll get good for myself,
And do good to others,
And try to help all,
As though they were brothers;
No matter what fashionable wine-bibbers say,
I'll teach total abstinence's the only safe way.

FIRST BOY AGAIN. A member of Congress
I'm intending to be;
Perhaps me Vice-President
You one day will see!
And if *I* help make laws
For this nation of nations,
Neither sailors nor soldiers
Will get *rum* with their rations.
And I'll do what I can
To lay by on the shelves
All the members who drink
And make fools of themselves.

ALL TOGETHER IN CONCERT.
True and earnest boys and girls
Who will work with a will
Can take a long step
Toward removing this ill.

A. SWASEY OBEAR.

YOUNG TEMPERANCE ORATOR.

CHARACTERS.—*Albert, John, Fannie, Jessie, Mr. Gordon.*

[*Albert and John enter and take seats.*]

JOHN. Well, Albert, I am really glad you have come back again; for you are usually the ringleader in all our sports, and we cannot spare you very well. But what is this? (*Takes hold of Al's coat-collar, and examines something.*)

ALBERT. That is a Band of Hope badge.

J. Band of Hope—that's a temperance society, isn't it?

A. Yes. Most of the young folks at Rosslyn Village, where I have been visiting, belong to it; and, believing it to be a good thing, I joined.

J. And signed the pledge?

A. Certainly I did.

J. Oh! my; and now what will you do for cider?

A. Do without it.

J. That's easily said, but not so easily done. What does your father say about it? I know he is opposed to signing the pledge. He thinks it is not manly to "sign away one's liberty."

A. He knows nothing about it yet. Mother thinks it best to keep him in ignorance at present. She is afraid he will be very angry.

J. I guess he will; but I think it would be better for him if *he* would sign the pledge himself. Now, Al, I don't mean any offence; but tell me truly, don't you believe your father takes his glass too often?

A. Yes, John, I have known it for some time, and it grieves me very much. I do hope he will see the danger that threatens him, and turn back before it is too late. And now, John, I have work to do, and I want you to help me. I'm going round among the boys and girls, and try how many names I can get toward forming a Band of Hope. Will you give me your assistance?

J. How can I, Al? You know father makes quantities of cider, and I like it as well as you do; and then, it does me no harm to drink it.

A. John, you think that my father loves liquor too well; *he* began by drinking cider, but very soon he wanted something stronger, and so will you, if you don't stop.

J. Well, Al, I'll think about it; and may be I'll join, if I can give up my cider. Have a cigar? Splendid brand. (*Offers one.*)

A. Thank you; I don't smoke now.

J. Does your pledge forbid it?

A. It prohibits the use of tobacco in any form.

J. Well, that *is* going the teetotal with a vengeance! But come, let's take a walk; it is too pleasant to stay indoors. (*Rises.*)

A. I have no objection, provided we do not go very far; I expect two of my cousins this morning, and would not like to be absent when they come. (*Exeunt.*)

[*Enter Fannie and Jessie.*]

FANNIE (*scornfully*). Well, I've heard enough to know that Mr. Albert has brought home some extra superfine notions with him. He's got so stuck up among his rich relatives that he can't even drink cider with us common people.

JESSIE. You are mistaken, Fannie. Albert is too sensible to get "stuck up," as you call it. I think he has done just what is right.

F. Oh! you always *were* on his side. Well, I mean to fix a plan that will make him ashamed of his nonsensical airs, and make some sport for us besides.

JES. What do you intend to do, Fannie?

F. Oh! you'll see soon enough. Just wait a moment. (*Runs out.*)

JES. I hope she will not do anything to wound Albert's feelings, he is so sensitive. At any rate, she won't get any help from me. I wish all the boys about here would stop drinking, chewing, and smoking; I'm sure I should like them better.

[*Enter Fannie, with glass supposed to contain cider, and a large piece of pasteboard with a string attached.*]

F. Now, Jessie (*placing the glass on table*), I wish you to help me hang this placard up against the wall. You can reach higher than I can. But don't look at the other side till it is up.

JES. I'll not help to do anything that will make Al feel badly. You must carry out your plans alone.

F. You are really mean, Jessie May! But I'll fix it, in spite of you. (*Stands on tip-toe, and tries to reach a nail placed very high, but fails.*)

JES. Ha! ha! that's good.

F. You need not crow quite so soon, Miss Jessie. I'll succeed, never fear. (*Stands on a chair, and makes another attempt, but fails.*)

JES. (*clapping her hands*). Ha! ha! ha! Try again, Fannie. *Don't* you wish I would bring you a long ladder?

F. (*angrily*). You just mind your own business! You never *could* help anybody out of a scrape. You wouldn't even prompt me yesterday when I missed that word in spelling, and so I had to lose my place in my class. But I know how to do. (*Places the chair near the table, and mounts the latter, and, by standing on the edge and reaching over, succeeds in hanging up the card. The side which she has kept concealed is turned over, and she descends from the table.*) There! how does that look?

JES. (*reading aloud*). "MR. ALBERT GORDON, *Great Temperance Orator!*" Did you mark that, Fannie?

F. Only the second line. You notice it is not done near so nicely as the other. Al's father marked the name the last time I was here, to label a box for him, but did not use it. But here he comes, and John with him. (*The boys enter.*)

A. How are you, cousins? I'm very glad to see you. (*Shakes hands, and John does the same.*)

F. (*bowing very low*). And we are very happy to meet so distinguished a gentleman. (*Takes his arm, and leads him to the table, facing the audience.*) I hope you will refresh yourself with the contents of that glass before beginning your great lecture. (*Albert turns from one to the other, confused and astonished; looks at the placard, and then at Fannie, who seems to enjoy his embarrassment.*)

A. Really—this is—

F. (*placing her hand behind his head, and bending it forward suddenly*). Bow to the audience. (*All laugh.*) Now we are ready to listen with profound attention. (*All take seats.*)

A. Well, my friends, since you *will* force this honor upon me, I will muster up my courage, and do the best I can. But first I must dispose of this. (*Takes up glass, and pours contents out of a window.*)

F. O Al! how could you waste that nice cider?

A. The meeting will please come to order. I came home from my visit with the intention of forming a Band of Hope, and this is a good time to commence. I am sure that all young folks should be teetotalers; for then there will be no danger of their becoming drunkards in after-life, if they will only be faithful to the pledge. Some of us have fathers who drink, and we may be able to persuade them to reform. Those who have temperate fathers and friends can help those who have not; and so we can all try and do some good, even though we are young. Now, who will join my Band?

J. I will, gladly.

JES. And so will I.

A. And *you*, Fannie?

F. O Al! I'm ashamed of myself. I fixed a plan to mortify you and make sport of you, and I am caught in my own trap; for you *are* a temperance orator, even if you are a young one. I will join your Band, and do all I can for the temperance cause.

[*Mr. Gordon, Al's father, enters.*]

MR. GORDON. And do you think I intend to let you little ones go ahead of me in your good work? Not I. I have heard everything since John and Albert first entered, and, thanks to my little temperance man, shall be a teetotaler from this moment. (*Lays his hand on Al's head.*) I am proud of you, my son.

J. Hurrah for Al and Mr. Gordon!

MR. G. Now let's give a good "hurrah" for your Band of Hope.

ALL. Hurrah! STELLA.

BOUND AND TIGHT.

CHARACTERS.—*Jim and Harry.*

JIM. Hallo, there, Harry! where are you bound?

HARRY. Bound? I'm not bound at all. I am as free as the mountain air.

J. Oh! pshaw! Why don't you answer me? You know what I mean.

H. I know what you say; and if that is not what you mean, then say it over again, and improve upon it.

J. What is the use to be always haggling over words? I never speak to please you.

H. Words, Jim, should be the expression of our thoughts; and if you speak what you do not mean, 'tis your own fault if you are misunderstood. We should be accurate in our speech and in our life.

J. Well, then, I'll try it on again. Master Harry, where are you going?

H. I am on my way to the hall of the Sons of Temperance—a place where I find good society, pure enjoyment, and the means of improving my mind and heart.

J. Sons of Temperance! Ha! ha! Well, go in. I'm bound for a time, at Bunker's saloon.

H. Yes, you are bound for a time. In this use of the word *bound*, I fear you are correct—*bound* by your attachment to bad society, by your love of unnatural and unhealthy excitement, and by your habit of using strong drinks.

J. That's putting it rather steep. I shall expect to hear you call me a drunkard the next time we meet.

H. I trust you will be disappointed in that, for I always intend to speak just as I mean; and to call you a drunkard would give me inexpressible pain.

J. But you do say that I am a slave to strong drink; that I cannot resist temptation, and am therefore *bound* to visit Bunker's saloon.

H. I think, if you are not thus bound, you are a very passive and foolish victim. You see what others are who have long frequented that place, and if you are ready and willing to be like them, you are the first young man I ever saw who could coolly and deliberately make up your mind to go the downward way to ruin.

J. Oh! nonsense! Can't a fellow go on a time occasionally, and not make a fool of himself? I never got drunk in my life.

H. No one can go on such a time as you had at Bunker's a week ago, and not be far gone in his folly.

J. What do you mean by that?

H. You say that you never got drunk; but did you not acknowledge to me the other day that you were a little tight?

J. Tight? Oh! that's nothing. Half the young fellows do hat.

H. And what is the exact difference between getting *tight* and getting *drunk?* Can you tell me?

J. Why, that is clear enough to be seen, but I don't know as I can express it to suit you.

H. Please do the best you can, for I really would like to know.

J. Well, I should say that the fellow who is *tight* is a little set up; while he who is *drunk* is a good deal set down.

H. Both, then, are in an unnatural state, and from the same cause. If he who is *set up* by liquor should drink a little more, he would be *set down*. Is that it?

J. Yes, I suppose that is about the fact of the case. We'll call it so, at any rate.

H. Then he who is *tight* is slightly drunk—that is, he has begun to be drunk. Do you agree to that also?

J. Why do you insist on the term *drunk?* That is a degrading and offensive word. I do not wish you to apply it to me directly or indirectly.

H. Have you not applied it to yourself? You say that he who is *tight* is a little drunk; and you acknowledge that a week ago you were a little *tight*.

J. I will not get offended, for I know you are my friend; but I confess that I do not like this attempt to degrade me by that offensive word. Why do you seek to force it upon me?

H. Because it belongs to you by your own decision. You are going in the way of evil men. You are in the incipient state of drunkenness. You are already bound (not hopelessly so, I trust) by a degrading habit, and I wish you to see your condition as it is. You do not like the name of *drunkard*, neither do I; but you are courting it, and it will be given you, whether you like it or not, unless you turn from the path in which you are now walking, and fly the danger which now threatens you. Jim, you do not look upon these things as they are. I love you, and therefore speak thus plainly.

J. I know you love me, Harry; and if any one else had said these things, I would have knocked him down.

There is to me a new thought in your words, and I will ponder it till we meet again. I shall not go to Bunker's to-day.

H. Thank God for that! Keep thinking, and you will soon find that it is best for every young man to be neither *bound* nor *tight*. Keep *free* from all bad habits, and in *temperance* and *sobriety* become what you *may* and *should* be—a respectable and noble man.

BOSTON NATION.

HOW TO MAKE ALL THE WORLD TEE-TOTALERS.

CHARACTERS.—*Tom and Bill.*

TOM. I say, Bill, you ought to have been at the lecture last night.

BILL. Of course I know I ought to have been there, if I could. But I couldn't; don't you see that? Father had a special job to finish, and I stayed at home to help him.

T. Well, you should have been there. It was jolly fun; and didn't he tell a crammer, that's all!

B. Who?

T. Why, the lecturer, certainly. What do you think he said? Why, he said if there was only one teetotaler in the world now, and he was to get one man to sign the pledge in a year, and then both of them got one each the next year, and so on, each getting one a year, everybody in the world would be a teetotaler in thirty years.

B. Did he say that for true?

T. He just did; and if that isn't a crammer, I don't know what is—ha! ha! ha!

B. But, Tom, may be the man was right after all. It may be true.

T. True! It can't be true. Why, look here. At the end of the first year there would be only two, wouldn't there? Then the second year, only four; third year, only eight. Why, it would be a thousand years making the world teetotal at that rate.

B. Stop a minute, Tom, I'll figure it out myself; lend me your lead-pencil, and I'll use the back of this envelope for a piece of paper. I'll keep on multiplying thirty times.

[*Bill industriously works at his figures, while Tom stands near, whistling and looking on.*]

B. Eureka! I've got it, and he *is* right. Just look here, Tom. I read the other day that the people in all the world were reckoned to be a thousand millions; and in thirty years, according to the lecturer's way of making them, there would be a thousand and seventy-three million, seven hundred and forty-one thousand, eight hundred and twenty-four teetotalers, and that's *more* than there would be people.

T. Nonsense, Bill; you're fooling!

B. Yes, there would; just look at the figures—1,073,741,824.

[*Tom takes the paper, and looks over it.*]

T. Well, I do declare, if it isn't right! I certainly thought it was a crammer, and the very idea made me laugh.

B. Then don't be in such a hurry next time to doubt what the lecturers say. But come, Tom, it is nearly school-time. Let's be off, and see if we can't fool some of the other fellows. At any rate, it is a first-rate hint for us all to go to work, and *each* one should do his share.

LITTLE BROWN JUG.

CHARACTERS.—*Ben Dorsey, drunkard; Albert and Lizzie, his children.*

(*Enter Ben Dorsey with brown jug in his hand. Dorsey sings:*)

"Ha! ha! ha! you and me,
Little brown jug, don't I love thee?
Ha! ha! ha! you and me,
Little brown jug, I *do* love thee."

(*Drinks from jug.*) That song was written in fun, I guess; but I can sing it in earnest. Little brown jug is all the comfort I've got now. Wife said she thought it was bad enough for me to break the pledge; but when I took to breaking the dishes, and some of them over her head at that, I suppose she couldn't stand it, so she took the children and went home to her mother, and I an't got nothing or nobody but little brown jug. (*Hugs it to his breast; sits down on floor, and leans against wall; drinks; sets jug beside him.*) I'm sleepy—guess I'll take a nap. (*Shuts his eyes.*)

(*Enter Albert and Lizzie, the latter walking on tiptoe, as if fearful of waking her father.*)

ALBERT. You needn't be so careful, Lizzie; he's dead drunk, I think. (*Scornfully.*) Now, an't that a great looking object to call father?

LIZZIE. Don't speak so, Albert; it isn't right.

A. Is it right for him to disgrace us, and treat us so badly we have to leave home? It's a hard-looking home, though; it was bare enough when we left, and now there isn't even a chair in the room; everything's gone for whiskey. We've tried to be good, obedient children, and yet he has brought us to poverty and disgrace; and, what is worse than all, he's just breaking mother's heart. Is that right?

L. (*distressed*). Of course it isn't right, Al; but he is our father, and we must do the best we can.

A. I think we've done the best we could for a long time. We've coaxed and begged him not to drink, and mother has cried until her beautiful eyes are dim; and what does he care about it? I believe he loves that hateful brown jug more than his wife and children. (*Takes cork from jug and smells contents.*) Phew! regular old benzine whiskey.

L. (*eagerly*). Let's empty it out, and fill it with water.

A. We'll do better than that; we'll empty it, and then smash it right here, as soon as he gets sober enough to know what we're doing.

L. (*alarmed*). O Albert! he'll just kill us, if we do that.

A. No danger of that; he is not very lively when he's just coming out of a spree; it's only when he's going *into* one that he's dangerous. Come on; let's spill this good liquor. (*Exit with jug, followed by Lizzie.*)

DORSEY (*opens his eyes*). So they thought I was too drunk to know what they were saying and doing; but they were mistaken. I tell you what, Ben Dorsey, your son has plenty of spirit and courage; and he's ashamed of his father, too, that's plain. How little Lizzie spoke up for me when he talked so scornfully! I *have* treated those children bad, but I never realized it so much before; and their mother—they say I am breaking her heart. Can that be so? Why, it has only been a short time ago that I would have made any sacrifice to save her a moment's pain; and she's been a loving, devoted wife. But why don't she come back to— Ah! here come the children; let's see what they will do.

[*Enter A. and L., the former bringing an old axe, and looking bold and determined; the latter with the jug, frightened and shrinking.*]

D. (*pretending to be angry*). You young rascals! what are you going to do? (*Lizzie screams and retreats a few steps.*)

A. (*bravely*). We're going to smash up this jug; and if you bring any more, we'll find them, and smash as fast as you bring them. Come on, Lizzie.

D. Smash my jug? Do it if you dare! You want to take away my only comfort.

L. Father dear, we and mother were your comfort before you got the jug, but that made you so bad we had to go away.

D. I'd like you to tell me what the jug made me do?

L. Don't you remember how the whiskey you drank out cf it made you beat mother and cut her head with a broken dish? And then you tried to throw Al out of the window.

A. And if Lizzie will push up her sleeve, you will see the great bruise where you struck her on the arm. (*Lizzie exposes her arm, on which a large purplish mark is seen. Dorsey looks at it, then covers his eyes.*) If you would stop drinking, you wouldn't do such things. You loved us once, father.

L. (*Drops jug, puts her arm around his neck, smooths his hair.*) If you *only would* promise to stop, father, and love us again!

D. (*with emotion*). I can't make any promises, child, I'm too weak; but you can do as you please with the jug.

A. Hurra! (*Kicks jug to front of stage; strikes it fiercely with the axe, till it is broken in pieces. Dorsey rises, and the three go out hand-in-hand, the children singing:*)

> "Ha! ha! ha! don't you see,
> Little brown jug, how we hate thee?
> Ha! ha! ha! don't you see,
> Old brown jug, we've done with thee?"

NELLIE H. BRADLEY.

LITTLE BESSIE.

CHARACTERS.—*Little Bessie, Bessie's Mother (a thoughtless woman), Mrs. Johnson, a teetotal neighbor.*

MOTHER. Bessie, where have you been all this time? Here I've been looking for you everywhere.

BESSIE. I've been to the Band of Hope, mother. There were plenty of ladies and gentlemen there; I wish you had gone too!

M. What do I want with ladies and gentlemen? You know I've no fine clothes to put on.

B. O mother! they speak so kindly, I'm sure it would do you good to hear them.

M. Are they any wiser than other people? What can they tell me that I don't know?

B. They would tell you about an enemy that is trying to rob people and take away their lives.

M. What enemy is that?

B. They said his name was alcohol.

M. What is alcohol?

B. They said it was that which got into people's heads and made them drunk, mother.

M. If that's all they've got to tell you at the Band of Hope, you sha'n't go any more. Do you hear me, now? (*Bessie hangs her head and wipes her eyes.*) What are you crying for?

B. O mother! do please let me go again. It is a very good place.

M. Not an inch shall you go again. I'll have none of their rooting into other people's business. Let them stay at home like me, and mind their own affairs. You go and bring me a bottle of beer!

B. O mother!—

M. Not another word, now; go, I tell you, at once. (*Bessie moves off.*) A fine thing, indeed, that a woman of my years must be taught what to drink and what to avoid by people who know nothing about it. They sha'n't dictate to me, however; I'll take care of that. Let everybody mind their own business, that's what I've got to say.

[*Enter Mrs. Johnson.*]

M. How d'ye do, Mrs. Johnson?

MRS. JOHNSON. I'm very well, thank you; how are you?

M. I'm as well as can be expected, considering what I have to endure.

MRS. J. Don't your husband keep sober now?

M. I'm sorry to say he does not. Last week he was off three days through drinking; and things are getting so bad with me, I'm sure I don't know whatever I must do.

MRS. J. What a pity he drinks so! I wish there was no drink!

M. It'll be the ruin of us all, ma'am, if he does not alter soon.

[*Enter Bessie with a bottle in her hand, stretching her arm out to keep the beer a long way from her mouth.*]

M. Who told you to carry beer that way, Bessie?

B. A gentleman at the Band of Hope said that if mother sent us for beer, we must keep the beer a long way from our mouth, lest we be tempted to drink.

M. I'll give you Band of Hope, if I catch you there again! Remember what I've told you, now. Put that beer away, and go tell Mrs. Roberts that I want to see her in the morning.

[*Bessie goes off, taking the bottle with her.*]

MRS. J. Don't speak so unkindly to your dear child.

M. I'll make her do my way, or else I'll see!

Mrs. J. But what if your way is not God's way?

M. I know what I'm doing. I go to church and read my Bible.

MRS. J. The Bible says: "Parents, provoke not your children to wrath, but train them up in the nurture and admonition of the Lord."

M. I said that she must not go to the Band of Hope, and she sha'n't.

MRS. J. Suppose, now, that near your house there were some dangerous rocks, and it was found that many persons had lost their lives by venturing too near the edge of those rocks; what advice would you give your child?

M. Why, I should say, "Bessie, you must keep a long way from the rocks; for if you go near them, you may fall over and be killed."

MRS. J. Did you ever hear of anybody being killed through drink?

M. Yes, scores. I've told my husband that drink will kill him some day, if he does not alter.

MRS. J. Just think, now, how thoughtless you have been. You admit that drink is like fearful rocks, on which many have lost their lives; you say the best way to avoid the danger is to keep away from the rocks; and yet you continue to drink yourself. Don't you see how you are putting yourself on the rocks? How can you expect to save your husband or preserve your child while you yourself are on the place of danger?

M. I never looked at it in that light before. What would you advise me to do?

MRS. J. Why, abstain, like I do. I can wash and bake and do all my house-work without strong drink. I have brought a family up without it, and you can do without it too, if you will try. Who can tell but that God will make you the means of rescuing your husband? Think what a comfort that would be. Then there is your dear child—

M. (*wiping her eyes*). God bless her! she is a good child. I'll not keep her from the Band of Hope.

MRS. J. She will be a comfort to you while you live, if you encourage her to do what is right.

[*Enter Bessie.*]

B. Mother, don't you feel well to-night?

M. Never mind, Bessie, I'll be all right soon.

B. Mother, we've learned such a beautiful song at the meeting to-night, and Mrs. Johnson knows it, too. May I sing it; and Mrs. Johnson, won't you help me?

MRS. J. Not to-night, dear; you can sing it for mother to-morrow.

B. Mother, you won't keep me away from the meeting, will you?

M. No, dear; you shall go as often as you like.

B. O goody! And won't you go with me next time?

M. You'll see, dear, when the time comes.

B. Mother, I've been praying for God to bless you and father, and—

M. (*sobbing*). God bless you, dear! I know why you prayed. Mrs. Johnson, have you got a pledge-book?

MRS. J. Yes, ma'am; come right across to my house and you may sign now.

B. Yes, do, mother; and then we both can pray that father may sign too. Sha'n't we be happy then, mother?

[*Exit.*]

QUESTIONS AND ANSWERS.

FOR TWO PERSONS.

Question.

DOES the butterfly ever get dry,
  As it floats on wings of golden hue?
It seems to think, when it lights on the pink,
  And the violet stored with dew.

Answer.

The butterfly soft, that soars aloft
  On its wings of gold and starry blue,

More than twice would think before it would drink
  Anything stronger than honey-dew.

Question.

The roses stirred when the humming-bird
  Dipped its bill in their fragrant bowl;
Does he put a drop in his rainbow crop,
  And dance and sing like a jolly soul?

Answer.

I give you my word that the humming-bird
  Is a teetotaler through and through;
If he puts a drop in his radiant crop,
  You know that he never gets blue.

Question.

The eagle that flies until lost in the skies
  Is so grand, so strong, and so swift;
Does he take anything to strengthen the wing,
  That sweeps like a cloud adrift?

Answer.

The eagle that soars where the thunder roars,
  And flies unafraid where lightnings gleam,
If he takes anything to strengthen his wing
  It is water that flows in the stream.

Question.

Some say that the deer will shed a soft tear
  From its mild and beautiful eyes;
Does it weep because it has broken the laws
  Which the moderate drinker defies?

Answer.

Oh! no, my sweet child; the red deer so mild
Only drinks from the river and lake;
Should you see a tear on the face of the deer,
Don't think that his pledge is at stake.

GEO. W. BUNGAY.

How it Paid.

CHARACTERS.—*Martin and George.*

[*Martin and George meet on the stage.*]

MARTIN. Well, George, I believe this is the first time we have met since we left school. What are you doing now?

GEORGE. I'm learning to be an engraver. My employer thinks I have considerable talent for that business.

M. How much pay do you get?

G. Five dollars a week is all I get at present. I have not been at work long enough to accomplish much; but Mr. Gray says that if I am patient and persevering, I shall be able to double it in the course of a year.

M. Five dollars a week! That don't pay. I get *nine*; and there is a situation of the same kind that you can get, if you'll apply right away.

G. What kind of a situation is it?

M. That of salesman in a large grocery and liquor store.

G. Do you have to sell the liquor?

M. Of course I do, just the same as anything else in the store.

G. Well, I'd rather work hard for five dollars where I am than to get ten where *you* are.

M. That's queer talk. I'd like to know the reason why?

G. Selling liquor is a mean business, whether you sell it by the pint or the barrel; and then, it's dangerous for any one, especially a boy, to handle the article. He might be tempted to taste it.

M. Suppose he does, is that a crime?

G. Not of itself, exactly; but you know that tasting too much makes people *commit* crimes very often. Of course it is not to be supposed that you ever will; but I should like to see you engaged at something else.

M. Something like you are doing, perhaps, at five dollars a week! No, I thank you; it wouldn't pay. I value my services at a higher rate. Good-evening!

G. Good-evening!

[*Exit in opposite directions.*]

Scene II.

[*George enters with newspaper in hand.*]

G. I can scarcely believe that Martin Day would be guilty of such conduct; yet here it is in black and white. (*Reads.*) "Martin Day, one of the young salesmen in Brown's grocery and liquor store, was arrested yesterday, charged with purloining fifty dollars from his employer's desk. The money was found in his pocket. His youth and evident penitence have induced Mr. Brown to decline prosecuting him, being content to discharge him with a severe reprimand."

[*Enter Martin with hat pulled over his eyes.*]

M. (*sullenly*). So you are reading the story of my disgrace?

G. O Martin! you cannot imagine how sorry I feel. Sit down, and tell me if it be true. (*Leads him to a seat.*)

M. Yes, it is all true, and more besides that was not published. One year ago you warned me, and I thought you were silly; but now I am a disgraced fellow, and all owing to that cursed liquor.

G. Stop, Martin! don't use such language.

M. Well, I won't do it again, if I can help it ; but when I think what liquor has done for me, I feel desperate.

G. How did it happen, Martin ?

M. It began just as you said, by tasting a little at first (there's a sample-room attached to the establishment, you know) ; and it has gone on from that, until I have often left the store with a very light head. Day before yesterday, the other clerk and myself were in that condition when we started home, and, before I was aware of it, I found myself in a gambling-saloon for the first time in my life. If I had been sober, I should have gone out as fast as possible ; but I was too much befogged to realize what I was about, and I was persuaded to take a lesson at the card-table.

G. You don't say you *gambled,* Martin ?

M. Yes, and lost all the money I had—nearly a month's salary. Yesterday I felt so miserable about it that I kept drinking slyly all day, until I was ready to do anything wicked. I took fifty dollars from Mr. Brown's desk, intending to win back my own money, and then return his secretly. It was missed before I had a chance to get away with it, and I was detected and discharged. If it were not for my mother and sister, I should feel like hanging myself. (*Drops his head on his hands, and groans.*)

G. (*laying his hand on his shoulder kindly*). You must not cherish such feelings, Martin. Begin again, and make for yourself a name for soberness, industry, and honesty that will cause all this to be forgotten.

M. (*raising his head*). Thank you for such encouraging words. I *will* try again, but not in this place ; no one would give me a chance to redeem myself here, nor would I ask it. I will go where I am not known, and will work my way up. And I tell you, George, I'll dig on the streets, or peddle old clothes, before I'll go to work in any establishment where liquor is sold. If I had only been content to begin as you did, I might, like you, be receiving fifty dollars a month now, and the same respect and confidence.

G. What do you propose to do now?

M. My brother-in-law has loaned me some money, and given me a letter of introduction to a friend in Baltimore, who will help me to find employment of some kind—something which has no associations of a nature to injure my morals and reputation. You shall hear an account of me soon that will make you feel proud of your old schoolmate; for I have learned this lesson: there's more to think of in any business than the dollars it brings. Some things *don't pay* at any price. I must be off. Good-by!

G. (*shaking hands*). Good-by, and success to you! (*Curtain drops.*)

STELLA.

THE NEW PLEDGE.

PRINCIPAL CHARACTERS.—*President, Secretary, Geo. Hoyt, Henry Faber, Jasper Clark, Edward King, and as many members as desired.*

[*A scene in the society room. President in chair, other officers and members in their places.*]

SECRETARY. George Hoyt is accused of breaking his pledge.

PRESIDENT. George, what have you to say for yourself?

GEORGE (*steps out and stands*). Not guilty.

PRES. Who is the first witness in this case?

SEC. Jasper Clark.

PRES. Jasper, please tell us what you know about it.

JASPER (*standing*). I was in at Mr. Townsend's last Saturday night, when George Hoyt and Eli Townsend came in all wet from eel-fishing. Mrs. Townsend brought out some cherry-brandy for Eli, and told him to drink it to prevent his taking cold; and she gave some to George, and he drank it.

PRES. What have you to say to that, George?

G. I took it as a medicine.

PRES. Were you sick?

G. No, but I was afraid I should be.

PRES. People generally wait till they are sick before they take medicine.

G. I thought if I took medicine to prevent my becoming sick, that would be still better.

PRES. But you did not take it by order of a physician.

G. The pledge does not require that.

PRES. Well, then, is every one to be his own judge?

G. He can be for all the pledge says to the contrary. But my pa says he would as soon trust Mrs. Townsend as any physician in the place, and much sooner than he would Dr. Lettson, who gets drunk every day.

PRES. If we can choose our doctors in that way, suppose we should all take the advice tipsy Jim gave us when he found us all shivering without a fire one evening, and take a little cordial to keep us from getting cold. Would you agree to that?

G. No; but I do not see that it would make much difference whether you took it by the advice of tipsy Jim or tipsy Dr. Lettson.

PRES. Let us look at it in another light, then. Suppose you were a reformed man—had once been a drunkard, like many of the men who are now members of temperance societies. Now, taking medicine of that sort would be the worst thing you could possibly do—serve you worse than a dozen colds. Don't you see that would not be a safe rule?

G. Yes, but I am not a reformed man.

PRES. True, but we want a society that will be safe for a reformed man or anybody else. We want no two rules about it.

G. Then why allow it for medicine at all, if it is not

safe for the reformed man to take it, and you want no two rules?

PRES. (*a pause*). Well I did not make the pledge. (*Another pause.*) What shall we do with this case? (*Looking around.*) Has any member anything to say about it? (*Another pause.*)

J. If we want a society where the reformed man and everybody else would be safe, and no two rules about it, why not have a pledge not to take alcoholic liquors at all for any purpose? If the reformed man can get along without them for medicine, we can; and do you not all think that it would be the best way?

HENRY FABER. I like that idea. It does seem to me that we are the safest not to tamper at all with anything that has done so much mischief and killed so many people. It was taking distilled spirits for medicine that first got the people to taking them for drinks.

EDWARD KING. But isn't it just possible that we might *need* to take them for something. Isn't such a step rather venturesome?

J. Not half so venturesome, to my notion, as it is to foster the idea that we need this terrible poison. My father says he has not taken a drop of alcohol in any shape for forty years, and I think I can do without it as well as my father has. Who will pledge with me for total abstaining?

E. I don't think it fair to change the pledge after you have got us all into the society.

H. We ought not to do that, of course, unless all agree to it. If they do not, there is another thing we can do. Those who wish to go in for "No Alcohol" put "N. A." after their name on the pledge-book. Here goes for my name. (*He writes in the book.*)

J. I'll agree to that. (*Signs.*)

G. That means something, and I like it. (*Signs.*)

H. I move that action in George's case be postponed indefinitely.

PRES. All in favor say ay.

ALL. Ay.

PRES. Secretary, please put N. A. after my name.

SEC. I will, and after my own too.

E. Here, I don't like to be left out in the cold. (*He takes the book and writes, and all the rest do the same. While they are writing, the colloquy proceeds.*)

J. Mr. President, I would like to ask Henry where he found this capital idea.

H. My grandfather told me that the first pledges of our temperance societies were against distilled liquors only, and not against cider, wine, and beer. But when they found these too would make drunkards, they began to take the pledge against them by writing "T. A." after their names, which means "total abstaining," and they did this until they had a total abstinence pledge. So I thought we could mend our pledge until we get a better by adding "N. A.," which means that we will not take the stuff at any time nor under any circumstances.

PRES. A capital idea, and I hope we will have a pledge like that very soon. All in favor of that rise and sing "God speed the Right." (*They all rise up and sing.*)

JULIA COLMAN.

THINGS WORTH KNOWING.

CHARACTERS.—*Tom, Dick, and Harry.*

TOM. Now, Dick, your father is a temperance man; mine an't. You are a Cadet and Hope Bander, and ought to know all about the cold-water cause. I want to ask you a question or two about Cadets, and Bands of Hope, and Sons, and Washingtonians.

DICK. Well, Tom, if I can answer your questions, I shall be happy to do so; go ahead.

TOM. How many years ago did the temperance cause start?

D. Why, Tom, the Bible speaks of men who drank no wine, and that must have been thousands of years ago.

T. I want to know when it began in this country?

D. I heard Dr. Jewett say, in one of his lectures, that it commenced here among white men about forty years ago; but before that time there was an Indian chief who called upon the law-makers in Ohio and Kentucky for a law to prohibit the sale of whiskey to the Indians. Jefferson was President of the United States at that time, and he joined with the chief in his efforts to put a stop to the sale of rum to the red men.

HARRY. How came our folks—I mean the white folks—to start the temperance reform?

D. Because there were so many persons, young and old, who drank to excess. Almost everybody drank beer and wine and whiskey, and all kinds of liquors. The people thought they could not work in the hay or harvest-field, in the warehouse or workshop, without liquors. Liquors were used when visits were made, and at weddings and funerals. They were placed upon side-boards, and passed around to the guests freely, and even the children were treated to liquors sweetened with sugar.

T. Were there no temperance men at that time?

D. Oh! yes; about that time that great and good man Gerrit Smith began to speak and write against intemperance, and thirty-five years ago he made a speech in the City Hall Park, New York, in favor of the disuse of distilled liquors. In New England, Dr. Lyman Beecher, Dr. Chapin, Dr. Edwards, Dr. Hawes, and other noble men preached against the great evils of drunkenness. Soon men like Dr. Jewett, Deacon Moses Grant, and many others took sides against the drinking customs.

H. How many people were there in the United States forty years ago—can you tell?

D. Yes, I have a temperance catechism at home, and that gives me all the dates and figures and facts. At that time there were about twelve millions of people in this country.

H. How much did they drink?

D. About seventy-five millions of gallons a year. That would be about equal to six gallons to each man, woman, and child.

T. Say, Dick, do you know when the first temperance society was formed in this country?

D. In 1826.

T. That is forty-four years ago, an't it?

H. Was that pledge like ours?

D. No; it was a pledge against the use of ardent spirits only. In 1832, another pledge was adopted, and that excluded wine, beer, and cider, and all kinds of intoxicating drinks. That is our pledge. We Cadets, and the Hope boys, promise also to abstain from the use of tobacco and profane speech.

T. I should like to know if people can get drunk on swearing or by chewing tobacco?

D. No; but boys and men who swear and chew are very apt to get drunk.

H. I know some good men who chew.

D. That may be, but they are none the better for chewing, and I think they would find it easier to be good if they did not chew.

G. W. BUNGAY.

www.ingramcontent.com/pod-product-compliance
Lightning Source LLC
LaVergne TN
LVHW010228110826
845151LV00004B/1219
* 9 7 8 1 4 2 5 5 2 5 9 3 4 *